__What Do Men Want From Women?_____

What Do Men Want From Women?

Robert Masello

For aught that I could ever read,
Could ever hear by tale or history,
The course of true love never did run smooth.

—A Midsummer Night's Dream
(act 1, scene 1)

Ballantine Books • New York

Published in the United States by Ballantine Books, a division of Random
House, Inc., and simultaneously in Canada by Random House of Canada
Limited, Toronto.

Portions of this book originally appeared in *Mademoiselle*

Library of Congress Catalog Card Number: 82-90842

ISBN: 345-30822-0

Manufactured in the United States of America

First Edition: May 1983

10 9 8 7 6 5 4 3 2 1

____Contents_____

____Introductory Remarks_

Already, I've got a problem. To whom should this book be dedicated? At 16, I promised my true love, Laurie, that someday I would grow up to be a great author and I would dedicate my first book to her, my only love and my sole inspiration. At 18, I seem to recall making a fairly similar promise to Betsy, during a heated clinch in the front seat of my older brother's Camaro. At 22, I had learned to save such announcements for more collected moments—I think I may have mentioned something to Alice about a dedication while we dawdled over the last of a bottle of chilled Montrachet, in a charming little bistro on Manhattan's Upper West Side. (If memory serves, that was the same night I casually tossed my linen napkin onto the tabletop when getting up to leave, without noticing that it had landed on the flickering candle. The napkin instantly went up like a torch, the waiter had to douse the flames with the water from the wine bucket, and Alice headed for the door like she'd never seen me before in her life. I doubt she remembers much about the dedication.)

Since then, I'm sure that I've promised to dedicate "my first book" to one or two other women who have captured my heart, and so, lest they be forever passing around the blame, I hereby dedicate it to them all. Which, in a way, is exactly right—all the women I have known, as friends (when I got lucky) or as sweethearts (when I got luckier) have contributed to it in one way or another. I have benefited or learned something from all of them. From Carol, how to make a Windsor knot in my tie. From Robin, how to read a roadmap. From poor Alice, how to neatly fold and replace my napkin on the table. With this book, maybe I can start to repay them, for those and much greater services.

My overall purpose here (besides earning enough to buy a co-op, an Exercycle, and a pair of pajamas that fit) is to explain, as best I can, today's single man to today's single woman. To provide, wherever possible, penetrating insights into the curious workings of the contemporary male psyche.

Such as why, for example, so many men promise to call, and then don't. Or why they so often vanish at the first sign of a serious commitment. Or what they do—and do not—want to hear in bed. At the same time, bold adventurer that I am, I plan to do a little exploring into the greater mysteries of love, life, and, of course, sex, that equally perplex both men and women.

For the past few years, that's pretty much what I've *been* doing, in a monthly column called "His" for *Mademoiselle* magazine. I've been talking to, and listening to, hundreds of men and women, discussing their social, sexual, and romantic problems and misunderstandings. I've also distributed hundreds of questionnaires soliciting comments and questions from single women all across the country. Not surprisingly, the same uncertainties crop up in El Paso, Texas, Ann Arbor, Michigan, and Great Neck, New York.

Which, depending on how you look at it, I suppose, is either something of a relief . . . or rather depressing. Think of it, for my sake, as a relief—otherwise, what would I have had to write about?

Part I

First Encounters, First Impressions

The Four Great Don'ts (or, How Not to Find True Love)

Sometimes, I think there ought to be a federal law against broadcasting certain commercials on Saturday night. As if I didn't feel bad enough already, sitting home watching the tube, the last thing I needed to see was a commercial that began "Alone? Lonely? A total reject?" or words to that effect. It was a spot for one of those computer dating services, and even though it failed to get me to call that magic number on my TV screen—"to meet that special someone just waiting for me"—it *did* start me thinking.

How *do* you go about finding a new partner in romance these days? There are lots of classic remedies—like singles bars, social clubs, ski trips. And there's certainly no dearth of books and magazines dedicated to building your self-esteem and sending you out on the scene again armed with new pick-up lines and a thorough knowledge of body language. But while some of these methods may work for some of the people, some of the time, for most of the people, most of the time, they're a total bust. Which is why I've decided to assemble here some of my own suggestions, culled from years of research and experience, for those of you on the prowl. I call them the Four Great Don'ts, and while observing them won't *guarantee* you'll leave the party escorted by the man of your dreams, ignoring them will surely mean pulling your own coat out of the heap on the bed and waiting at the bus stop by yourself.

Don't Wear New Underwear to a Party. There's something fatally optimistic about putting on brand-new underwear, something about crisp elastic and unfrayed fabric that terribly offends the gods who preside over sudden, serendipitous romance. Before going out sometimes, I used to unwrap a new pair of snappy underpants, thinking idly, expectantly, hopefully, that this might prove important before the night was through. That the next morning, padding around some strange woman's apartment, I might be glad I had such handsome, intact underwear on, underwear that proclaimed me to be, in every way and layer, a prosperous, tidy guy.

Needless to say, my new underwear has never been so displayed.

In fact, you could count on the fingers of one hand the number of nights I've set out on the prowl and wound up anywhere other than alone in my own little bed. And on the few occasions when I did meet up with unforeseen passion, I invariably had on the most ragged, ridiculous underwear I owned. Once it was a pair colorfully emblazoned with the license plates of all 50 states (a joke gift from my mother) and another time it was a dilapidated pair of thermal long johns, too short in the leg and too wide in the waist. Both were capable of converting lust to laughter, ardor to ambivalence, in record time.

Don't Clean Up Your Apartment Before Going Out. This precaution is, in fact, a corollary to the one above. It works on the same principle: Whatever you do that expresses optimism about the outcome of the evening, that openly advertises your hope of finding someone so special, so right, that you'll simply fall into each other's arms a split-second after meeting, will doom you to failure right off the bat. (Those spiteful gods again.) How many nights have I carefully smoothed the bedspread, finished the dishes in the sink, stuffed all my dirty clothes in the laundry bag, and deposited a bottle of dry white wine in the refrigerator to chill, before setting out to find the love of my life? And how many nights have I returned home to mess up the bed myself, and drink a solitary toast to the *Late Late Show*? It's somehow infinitely more disheartening to come home to a spic-and-span apartment than a messy one, to the evidence of your best-laid plans and fond hopes, now so clearly quashed. In fact, it's downright embarrassing (even if there isn't anyone but you around to witness it).

Don't Go Out Alone. This piece of advice may sound strange at first; after all, why should you be running around if you've already got someone to be with? But when I say "don't go out alone," I mean take a friend with you—ideally one in the same situation as you (lacking the perfect paramour). And it doesn't matter if your companion is the same sex or the opposite—either way it's a good idea to have someone else along on the expedition.

Why? There are a few good reasons. For one, if things don't go well, it keeps you from standing by yourself in the corner, staring despondently into your glass. There's nothing like appearing to be a wallflower or social pariah to ensure that you'll be treated as one. So long as you look like you're in the swim, you have a chance of *being* in the swim; and without your friend to act as an occasional life preserver, it's easy to drown in a party crowded with strangers, or a noisy, dark bar.

If your friend happens to be of the opposite sex, so much the better. From my own experience, I can say that, for whatever mysterious reasons, I'm a lot more attractive to women at parties when I'm accompanied than when I'm alone. Not only is it easier to meet new women, but they seem much more comfortable talking to me. Maybe it's because I'm less threatening that way—a woman can relax and have a conversation without worrying about what will happen next, whether I'll make an unmistakable pass, whether she's giving me signals that I might misinterpret. Because I'm already "taken," she can explore a little more deeply without committing herself in any way; if I come up with the wrong answer at some point, she can simply walk away. And if I should happen to come up with all the right ones, well . . . there's always another day.

Or, for that matter, *that* day. Assuming you have a clear understanding with your traveling companion, you can always confess to your new-found love that you're unattached, and take it from there. But do be sure that you and your friend *have* agreed ahead of time that it's every man for himself and that you won't necessarily be leaving the party together. I can recall wading through a packed discotheque for an hour in search of my friend Cathy to tell her I felt like leaving. I never did find her, and it was only when she got in touch a week later that I discovered she'd left with her own Prince Charming about ten minutes after we'd arrived.

The final "don't" is by far the most important of all, but it's also the hardest to follow. It's simply this: *Don't* want *a new relationship*. They say that dogs can smell fear; I don't know how much truth there is to that, but I do know that people can sense desire, a longing for intimacy, for love. And that perverse as it may be, the more keenly you want to meet someone new, the less likely you are to manage it. People are attracted not to need or loneliness, but to independence and strength. And the more confidence and contentment you display, the more attractive you'll be.

On the tennis court, to make what may seem an unusual analogy, I have the same sort of problem, but in a somewhat different guise. During the warm-up volleys, I'm relaxed, having fun, taking chances on some riskier shots. But the moment the match starts, I become tense, stiff, unwilling often to make anything but the defensive play. As a person, I'm much happier—and more pleasant to be around—during those earlier volleys, when I'm not so intent on the outcome. And I also happen to play a much better, more interesting and effortless style of tennis. Social games, I think, should be approached in the same relaxed, casual manner. Go in with smaller expectations: just plan on having a good time. If you meet someone truly special, great; you've outsmarted the vengeful gods. If not, just think how relieved you are that you didn't go to the trouble of buying new underwear, or cleaning your apartment, for no good reason.

___Three Good Do's
(or, How to Find True Love)__

Unfortunately, even the messiest apartment, dirty dishes stacked to the ceiling, dust balls the size of armadillos (how big are armadillos, anyway?) won't guarantee that you'll find true love. Sometimes it takes more than general slovenliness and disarray to do the trick. Sometimes, it takes some good, hard, common sense.

I think, most immediately, of my own older brother, Steven, a warm, witty, outgoing fellow who, nonetheless, spent most of his early adulthood sans date. Charming as he could be at a family gathering, or even a party, as soon as it came down to calling someone up and asking her out, his tongue tied itself into knots, his hands became numb, his eyes appeared to glaze over. On at least three occasions, we thought he had slipped, irreversibly, into a catatonic state.

But he was not—and he'll kill me when he reads this—without desire. Many's the night I remember him combing his hair, tucking in his shirt and heading off for one of the popular bars in downtown Chicago. As soon as he was out the door, my parents and I would fall to our knees and *pray* that this time would be different, that he would meet someone, someone nice, and friendly, and attractive. And every time, when he returned a few hours later, he would be wearing the same morose expression, and announce, in bitter, disillusioned tones, "I can't stand the kind of girls who go to singles bars."

If my brother's problem weren't such a common one, I wouldn't have bothered to bring it up. But it is, I think—in his loneliness and desperation, he'd managed to completely lose sight of what it was he truly wanted and needed. He was just doing the obvious—going to singles bars—in the almost impossible hope that the woman seated on the next stool would be all he'd ever dreamed of (*and* that she'd lean over and tell him so). He was searching for a soul-mate, a loving and loyal companion, someone to share his interests in Elizabethan poetry and Italian opera, in some of Chicago's noisiest and most impenetrable singles bars. It wasn't really "the kind of girl who goes to singles bars" he was objecting to—it was the crowded, loud "meat market" atmosphere, which renders everyone, men and women alike, equally un-intelligible and superficial. Not that that made his lack of success there any less rankling, I suppose.

What my brother, like a lot of other people in his situation, failed to do was, first of all, to define his objective, and then to figure out how best to achieve it. If that sounds sus-piciously like a military strategy, well, maybe that's not so far wrong. In love as in war, knowing what you're after, and the fastest way to get there, is half—if not all—of the battle.

In a moment of tranquility, not a Saturday night when the blood is racing and the hormones are high, sit back and con-sider, calmly and rationally, what kind of man you're looking for. Is he quiet, kind, a bespectacled intellectual? Or a rug-ged, brawny pioneer, the kind of guy who can't really enjoy his dinner unless he's killed it himself? Are you looking for someone with whom to go antiquing in the Pennsylvania countryside, and enjoy a candlelit supper in an eighteenth-century inn? Or do you want somebody with a green, Mo-hawk hairdo, who'll dance your feet off, then whisk you back to his Soho loft for an all-night orgy of body painting and nitrous-oxide inhalation? These are all, as you may have no-ticed, fairly different, and distinct, types, and while you don't necessarily have to define your quarry quite so precisely, it does help when you know at least which direction you're going in.

Especially because that will also tell you where to go to find him. If you're looking for the studious sort, don't book yourself into Club Med in Guadeloupe for a week—join a poetry-reading club, or lurk in the stacks at a local library. If it's Mr. Party you want, then buckle on your dancing shoes and immerse yourself in the thick of the nightlife. I realize how elementary some of this counsel may sound, but that's probably why it's so often overlooked, or ignored.

If you're really feeling devious, you can steal a page from my friend Lisa's book. One evening, she confessed to me, in strictest confidence, her own secret method for meeting likely prospects. "I just place an ad in the *Times*, offering for sale something like an antique musical instrument, or a col-lection of rare hunting prints. Men who are interested in things like that are the kind of men that I'm interested in, and if, over the phone, they sound like someone I'd like to meet, I invite them to come over the next day. Of course, once they get here, the antique violin, or the print collection, or the vintage Porsche, has either already been sold, or been repossessed by my crazy old aunt, who's just decided she can't live without it after all. I make profuse apologies, offer a drink, and see what happens from there. It ain't foolproof, but it's not a bad way to beat the bushes."

"Has it ever led to any serious relationships?" I asked.

"Once, and once I got some very lucrative freelance work out of it. But I tell you, if I had some antique Porsches for sale, I'd be set for life."

If steps one and two consist of pinpointing your target and his probable whereabouts, step three is making sure that what you've pinpointed is a real-live possibility, someone who could conceivably exist within the realm of all previous human experience. If, for example, you're looking for a man with the body of Arnold Schwarzenegger, the wit of Woody Allen, and the money of an Arab sheikh, you may be asking for something that's impossible, or at least extraordinarily difficult, to find. You may, in fact, be asking for one man in whom almost totally contradictory qualities reside. It took me years to figure it out, but that was exactly what my friend Beth kept doing wrong.

Almost three years ago, she was dating a guy named Gary, who was, even if I say so myself, quite a catch. A good-looking entrepreneur, in his early 30s, he made more in a day than I make in a year—even a good year—and owned a duplex on Park Avenue, a beachhouse in the Hamptons, and the midnight blue Mercedes 450 SL, with wire wheels, black leather upholstery, and Blaupunkt sound system, that I had often dreamt of, on my most idle afternoons. But what made me hate him even more was the fact that I liked him—he was without a doubt the most personable millionaire I know.

Beth liked him, too. She also liked the weekends at his summer house, the box seats at the ballet, the leisurely drives through the streets of Southampton, in what—if there were a god in heaven—would have been my car. She admired his success, his ambition, his sophistication. But as time went by, she appeared to discover a serpent in her Eden.

"I mean, it's great to be going out with such a dynamo, who's wheeling and dealing 24 hours a day, all over the country. It's great to find a 12-ounce bottle of Joy on your desk at the office, or a dozen long-stemmed roses waiting at your door. But I miss having someone who can be with me every night for dinner, somebody that I can call in the middle of the afternoon just to chat about lots of little things, some-

Three Good Do's—9

body who would be content to sit on the bed, with a bowl of popcorn, and watch David Letterman before falling asleep. I need more attention, more cuddling and simply being together, than Gary can give me."

Which to me, and most of her other friends, sounded understandable. If that's what Beth wanted, then that's what she should have. And being the bright, attractive person that she is, it didn't take long before she was dating someone she'd met at the advertising agency where she works, a market researcher who worshiped the carpet she walked on, who wanted nothing more than to be at her side both night and day, who not only joined her for dinner every night but generally cooked it to boot. He did prefer granola bars to popcorn, but that didn't seem like an insurmountable obstacle.

And for the next five or six months, everything seemed to be just fine. The market researcher was spending almost every night at Beth's place (presumably watching David Letterman and munching on granola bars), he was showering her with affection, he was seriously committed to the relationship. He would even call her during the afternoon—his office was on a different floor—just to swap the trivial news of the day. So imagine my surprise when Beth and I met for lunch, on one of those rare days when I'd gotten up in time, and she announced to me that she couldn't take the relationship anymore and wanted out.

"He's a perfectly nice guy really, and I wish him well. He's just not for me. I mean, he'd be perfectly content to work as a market researcher for the rest of his life, just one more cog in the huge, corporate machinery. He hasn't got enough oomph for my tastes; I like a man who's more aggressive and independent and ambitious, somebody who's more take-charge, who's got bigger goals. I can't love a man unless I can respect him first, and I just don't think I can respect him—and this is probably terrible of me to say—unless he's successful. In fact, the more successful, the better."

When I blearily suggested, between gulps of hot coffee, that she had just described her previous sweetie, Gary, she looked at me blankly for a moment, and then said, "Boy, you must really be still asleep. You remember what the problem was with Gary—he was always too wrapped up in his work to pay enough attention to me."

Groggy as I was, still I was able to detect the rumblings of some nearly irreconcilable requests here. What Beth wanted was an ambitious young success story, who'd somehow still have all the time and energy necessary to lavish affection and attention upon her. She wanted a guy who was aggressive, strong-willed and independent, but who'd enjoy kibbitzing on the phone in the afternoons, and pursue an almost symbiotic relationship with her. She wanted a man who would openly, avowedly, doggedly declare his love for her—as did our friend in market research—but she didn't realize that as soon as he did so, she'd almost immediately begin to lose interest in him. What she was asking for was a kind of superman, who, if he existed at all, was probably booked solid every night through 1989.

It's not that sensitive, loving millionaires can't be found. (I think I read in *National Geographic* that one was recently spotted by plane in the Nepalese bush.) It's just that the qualities needed to make a dynamic and successful young entrepreneur are generally at odds with the qualities that comprise the tender, attentive homebody sort. I won't go so far as to claim that they're mutually exclusive, but I will say that terribly compatible they're not.

Like a lot of people (myself included, most of the time) Beth hadn't really sorted out her priorities and her needs. She hadn't accounted for her own ambivalence—was the chase more fun than the capture, were success and its glamorous trappings more appealing to her than a solid, workaday relationship?—or her own insecurities, which made her instinctively, and irrationally, devalue anyone who offered to give the love she was looking for. Like Groucho Marx, who wouldn't join any club that would have him as a member, Beth unconsciously discounted anybody who would settle for her. To her fundamental problem—impossible expectations—she'd added unresolved doubts about herself and what she really wanted in life. She broke up with Mr. Market Research about a month after our lunch (around the same time I finally woke up) and the last time I spoke to her, she was involved with a middle-aged psychiatrist, who, she told me with uncommon cruelty, is also driving my Mercedes 450 SL. There is no justice in the world.

___Expectations...and Reality: New Skills of the Single Man___

This business of expectations is an awfully tricky one for men these days. There isn't any clear-cut definition of what constitutes manly deportment anymore, no easy, step-by-step set of instructions to follow. Back in the Golden Age, a man had only to pillage, rape, and plunder to the best of his abilities in order to ensure himself of a respected place in the community; a chariot laden with booty was also considered a moral encomium. And even in much more recent times, men have been free, indeed encouraged, to exercise staggering insensitivity, ruthless ambition, and callous self-concern in their daily affairs (*and* their nightly ones). Getting ahead, getting even, getting to the top, simply *getting,* was the name of the game, and as such not very hard to comprehend; mastery was what took some luck and effort. But in the past decade or two, much of that has at long last changed—those appealingly simple and straightforward dictums just don't cut the ice any longer. In both big things and small, today's man has to be a lot more versatile and original than his predecessors (those lucky stiffs). Like any other species threatened with extinction by a suddenly altered environment, he has had to adapt himself to the brave new world of liberation, to gently nudge awake portions of his brain that have lain happily dormant for as much as millenia.

The message was brought home to me with special impact one recent afternoon when I was suiting up in the locker room of a local athletic club. Right beside me were these two strapping hulks, deeply engrossed in conversation. Well, expert eavesdropper that I am, I figured I was sure to overhear some valuable stock tip, some raunchy sexual escapade, or at least a little hot-blooded political debate. But five minutes later, when I dejectedly left the locker room, all I had managed to pick up was a recipe for a perfectly wonderful Veal Marengo, along with a few helpful hints on how to blanche asparagus and assorted other vegetables. (Too small a pot, apparently, and you spoil them.)

But, really—Veal Marengo? I can remember a time when no man in his right mind would even have admitted eating it, much less cooking it. Men ordered steak—raw—and in the locker room, they discussed the Superbowl and the Dow Jones Industrial Average. If they could light a barbecue (always a male preserve) with the very first match, they were acclaimed as consummate chefs.

Not so, anymore. That culinary instinct, probably last in evidence at the Saturday night mastodon roast, has lately had to spring back into action. Gone forever are the days when a man could successfully do his wooing over a greasy pizza from the corner. Now if I have a woman over for dinner, I have to make absolutely sure that my James Beard is left open, and dog-eared, on the counter, that my spice rack takes up most of one kitchen wall, and that no telltale Bird's Eye boxes are poking their flaps out of my garbage bag (now efficiently nestled in a white, foot-pedaled receptacle). I have to say things like, "I think the kitchen is my favorite room," frequently take a taste from a long-handled wooden spoon, and swear I'd kill for an espresso machine. I also have to painstakingly gather up all the take-out menus that normally litter the tables, desk, and floor, and hide them under the mattress. If my American Express bills weren't as high as they already are, I'd never even *conceive* of having someone over for dinner.

Nor would I think of allowing anyone to witness what might be called, with wild generosity, my decor. At one time, it was naturally assumed that a man's apartment would be a mess, furnished with mismatched furniture, shredded shower curtains, worn-out throw rugs; it was even thought kind of winning, according to many cultural anthropologists. But that, too, has all changed, and today's man is expected to know and observe at least some of the rudimentary rules of decorating and household maintenance.

In my own apartment, that has entailed reupholstering the rocking chair I inherited from my grandmother, replacing the reading lamp I hit with a Wiffleball bat in college, and once every summer, stepping out on the fire escape with a bucket and a sponge to wash the front windows. For many of my friends, it has meant even more than that. Gerald, a publishing exec, last month redid his place from top to bottom; the only thing his girlfriend still objected to was the framed photograph of Bo Derek over the mantelpiece. Ralph went totally High Tech (I think his apartment's about as comfortable as the inside of a toaster now), and Peter, a professional guitar-ist who until a short time ago thought that his socks, ran-domly strewn around the room, provided a kind of festive color accent, recently picked them all up. In fact, the last time I was over there he proudly displayed to me his brand-new, "Desert Dawn" wall-to-wall carpeting, teak platform bed, glass-topped coffee table, sleek, modern bureau, and Japanese drawstring window shades. He even had the nerve to suggest that the curtains and bedroom carpeting at my own place clash. Clash!—this from the man who used to wear plaid trousers with a Madras jacket whenever he wanted to look really nice.

Not that he'd ever commit that same mistake today. His walk-in closet (formerly a graveyard for retired guitars) is now a veritable haberdashery, containing stacks of small-col-lared shirts, racks of skinny ties, sports coats, Shetland sweaters, and three—count 'em, three—Giorgio Armani suits. The days when a man could get by looking rumpled and un-color-coordinated have also passed; sloppy isn't cute anymore. Gerald, of the Bo Derek photo, has been looking like a Brooks Brothers ad of late, and Ralph, my High Tech friend, has taken to tweedy jackets, bow ties, and smoking custom-made tobacco blends in those curved, Sherlock Holmes-style pipes. (Clearly, a divided personality.) As for me, I've finally thrown out my two-toned bucks (the ones with the hole in the toe), I've had the lapels on my blue blazer narrowed, and I've bought all new underwear (which, if you've been reading this book straight through from front to back, you'll know I never wear when I'm out on the prowl).

...And His New Grievances

But those are the easy changes to make—learning how to whip up a soufflé, or iron a pair of pants, is a cinch compared to the more complex and confusing adaptations that men have got to perform these days. In the absence of any precise definition of masculinity, men have been looking to women for clues as to what will or will not go down now, what behavior will or will not be tolerated, what qualities should be cultivated and which ones tossed overboard. In an odd way, our social climate today bears an uncanny resemblance to one of those lab experiments, in which a pigeon is trained to earn his birdseed by pecking only at a green light; every time he does, he gets a pellet. If he mistakenly pecks the red light, instead, he gets a mild electric shock. For the experiment to succeed, however, with pigeons or with men (and there the comparison will end) the reinforcements have to remain constant—pecking the green light has *got* to yield a reward, pecking the red one has *got* to mean trouble. At the risk of beating a dead pigeon, I would merely like to suggest that much of the misunderstanding between men and women today may have come about because those lights have *not* been consistent; our experiment has *not* been performed right.

For instance—men are encouraged today to be more open, sensitive, loving, and vulnerable than at any time in the past. We are told it's okay to cry, to express our emotions; we are assured that donning an apron to help wash the dishes in no way detracts from our masculinity—that, if anything, it enhances it, by showing how surely we have risen above those silly old macho notions that still hold our most benighted comrades in thrall. In theory, we are praised for warmth, tenderness, caring—but in practice, we are often rewarded for quite different behavior.

Take, for instance, my own relationship with a woman I'll call Carol. Never in my life had I been so in love, never in my life had I been so sweet, so thoughtful, so helpful around the house. And yet, the more I pitched in, the more loving and attentive I was, the less interested she seemed to become in me. Her amorous inclinations, in particular, flagged noticeably. What made matters even worse was my discovery that as I withdrew, in a mixture of confusion, doubt, and anger, she seemed to suddenly revive. The colder and more aloof I became, the more excited and romantic *she* got. Before long, I discovered that I could consciously manipulate the situation, that I could often get by guile what I hadn't been able to get by more honest means. Like a fisherman on the verge of losing his catch, I could suddenly pull back hard on the rod, and reel her in that way. The only problem was that I hated fishing.

So do most of my friends—and yet, if I tell them that story, they can almost invariably match it with one of their own. In fact, I wonder if women have any idea how confusing men often find the signals they're getting, how garbled the message. We're respectfully requested to behave in a certain fashion, and then when we do, we find that somehow or other we've now lost most of our former allure. And what's even more galling, what really drives most decent, law-abiding men right up the wall, is that the guys who have gone right on behaving in a positively Cro-Magnon manner have also continued to attract more women than they know what to do with.

"That's what kills me," says Gerald, my publishing friend, who also considers himself one of the New Age men. "When I see these terrible guys making out like banshees, I think, 'Why do I ever bother to be nice? Why don't I just start acting like these Conan the Barbarian types? It doesn't seem to do them any harm.'"

Ralph (my High Tech friend) gets easily worked up about this subject, too—but then he has special reason. For the past six months, he's adored another young lawyer who works at his firm, but she, in turn, adores a junior v.p. at a huge, midtown bank. "I've been introduced to this guy," says Ralph, "and I think I can say, fairly, objectively, impartially, that he's a schmuck. He's got one of those pinched-up little faces, with no lips."

When I asked if the guy's lipless state was all the evidence Ralph had to go on, he nearly went berserk.

"Evidence? You want evidence? Just come to my office some morning and listen to Nancy herself bitch about him, about how he stands her up on dates, about how he ridicules her opinions, how he drones on and on about the petty politics at the bank, as if anyone else in his right mind would care. She's the first to concede that the guy treats her like dirt. But what did she do last Wednesday, ten minutes before we were supposed to go to lunch together? She cancels. Why? (Ralph is a master of the Socratic monologue.) Because Eugene—that's his name, if you can believe it—decided *he'd* be able to spare her an hour. And what did they talk about? Eugene. And Eugene's chances for a promotion at the bank. And Eugene's difficulties finding a co-op. According to Nancy, he didn't even notice that she'd had her hair cut in a totally different style—which, I might add, looks great on her. I guess to notice he'd have had to take his nose out of his soup bowl."

But why, you may wonder, are these men so wrought up? Why should they care who these women choose to go out with? Is it any of their business?

Indirectly, I'd say, maybe it is. What these friends of mine are venting, even if they don't know it, is a sense of betrayal; they feel, however obscurely, that they've agreed to play the social game by the new rules, the rules carefully laid out by liberated women everywhere, but that the women themselves, surprisingly enough, aren't always playing that way. They feel a little foolish, as if they've been duped, and, I think, they also feel a little defenseless, now that they've been persuaded to lay down the arms which men have traditionally employed in the age-old battle of the sexes. They've begun to feel themselves neither fish nor fowl, some uneasy hybrid between the old man and the new, an unsuccessful cross-breeding of Tommy Tune with Attila the Hun. They're angry with the men whose shenanigans continue to earn their entire sex a bad name, and they're even angrier with the women who conspire, consort with, and then turn around and complain about, these same incorrigible louts.

Great as the changes were that the women's movement brought about, some things, such as my father, remained impervious to its effects, by and large. So did a fair number of women. While subscribing wholeheartedly to its aims and principles, on some deeper level they hadn't yet completely come around. They knew, for example, what they were supposed to want in a man, but that wasn't necessarily what they *did* want. They knew they were supposed to be looking for an equal, but in fact, I think many women sought out men they could still consider a superior in some way—and there have always been plenty of men around ready, willing, and able to go along with such a notion. Loudly as they may have proclaimed their pride and unity and independence, many women weren't at heart utterly convinced of it themselves. How could it really have been any other way? Overnight, our laws can change, our lives can change, even our ideas can change, but to alter our fundamental, personal impulses and attitudes, all that stuff that's planted in us and inexorably grows from the moment we first draw breath, well, that takes a good deal longer.

In the meantime, while we're all waiting for that mendacious stuff to wither away, all that cant about the "clinging little woman" or the "independent he-man," my friend Gerald has his own idea of how to mollify the essentially decent, but frustrated men of America. "All I want," he says, "is a signed statement from the women of America, acknowledging their own complicity in at least some of our current sociosexual woes, and officially declaring men to be only part of the problem. I want to be able to frame and hang on my wall an official document—and I want it notarized—absolving men of at least *some* of the guilt and responsibility for all the present turmoil."

And what if they won't sign?

"If they won't sign, if they won't admit that they're aware of, and working on, major problems—like their fatal attraction to creeps and barbarians—then I'm afraid I cannot answer for the consequences," he hints, darkly. "But there's a chance—not a good one, but a chance, mind you— that after years of being the quintessential nice guy I may throw in the towel and 'go Conan' myself . . . I think they should think that one over."

The Vanity of
the Male Animal

Recently, I made the fatal mistake of checking into a hotel room with a full-length mirror on the back of the bathroom door. My own apartment has only one small, mirrored medicine chest, made even more useless by the extremely feeble overhead light. But here in this large, spotless hotel bathroom, there was not only a full-length, fully-polished mirror, but that harsh, relentless, brutally honest kind of lighting that makes your every pore a separate kingdom, light that turns your skin a phosphorescent combination of weak green and pale purple, that highlights every flaw, bulge, scar, and congenital anomaly. I had just stepped out of the shower stall when I happened to glimpse myself in all my glorious entirety, and without going into graphic, personal detail, suffice it to say I decided from that day forward never to go out in public again.

Well, of course, I *did* go out again (just three weeks later). But the reason I mention all this is just so no one will ever doubt the depth and the profundity that male vanity, like its female counterpart, can attain. We read every day about how concerned women are with their physical appearance, particularly signs of aging. But lately I've noticed, among my male friends and including yours truly, an ever-increasing obsession with our corporeal selves. With things collapsing, falling out, expanding, with the loss of the lithe, firm figures that not so very long ago we cut so gracefully in the world. Not to mention the stamina with which we were able, effortlessly and with impunity, to pull all-nighters, or consume whole pizzas at a single sitting. I never understood until recently my father's bedtime Alka-Seltzer. Now I don't understand how I've lived so long without it.

But what, you may ask, tops the list of these physical frettings, these anatomical betrayals that plague the young-enough-but-getting–up-there men of America? Without a doubt, the age-old pot belly heads up the dismal parade. I first went public with the issue in a phone conversation with my friend Peter about a year ago.

"You know," I said, "I really think we ought to start playing squash again."

"How come?" he asked.

"Because Robin was here this weekend, and when I got out of bed to adjust the TV set she told me I looked like I'd swallowed a bowling ball."

His riotous laughter was indelicate to say the least, I thought. "You're kidding? Not two weeks ago," he confessed, "Cheryl caught me sitting on the bed naked, with my legs crossed, and she told me I looked like one of those fat, little ivory Buddhas."

That made things much better. Now we routinely discuss the ebb and flow of our budding bellies, and what I've come to think of as the "boa constrictor effect." To wit: after consuming one of my customarily gargantuan dinners, perched on the bed and watching Dan Rather, I slump backwards against the pillows to drowsily observe the rhythmic rise and fall of my rounded tummy. Sometimes, I even think I can detect there the vague outlines of the chicken, pork chops, or whole ox I've just devoured.

An interesting outgrowth of this problem, which Peter and I have also discussed, is the need to present our rebellious bodies only in the most favorable lights and poses now. Where once I kept a three-way bulb in the bedside lamp, I now have a simple 75 watt'er. And Peter admits that although he used to bounce around pretty freely, a blithe and uninhibited spirit, "now I keep a robe handy whenever Cheryl's over for the night, and I try not to appear in profile too often. And I *never* sit on the edge of the bed with nothing on anymore."

"That one I don't get."

"Haven't you ever checked out what sitting on the edge of a bed does to your body? It makes so many folds in your abdomen that you look like an accordion. It's an extremely depressing sight."

Other problem areas? Women worry about gray hairs—men worry about no hairs. And it's more than just checking the old hairbrush on occasion to see how much it's collected lately. I have a friend from college, Herb, who's already begun to arrange his few remaining strands in laboriously plotted-out, schematic patterns; the topiary at Versailles never received so much attention. And another friend, Fred, just a few years older than I am, whose head, for the entire lengthy duration of his hair transplant, bore an alarming resemblance to the canal network on the surface of Mars.

But please don't think me smug—I'm doing okay in the

hair department so far, but I keep on my dresser a photo of my maternal grandfather, bald as the proverbial billiard at the age of 30. Supposedly, that's the best genetic indicator of how your own head will fare (or so some malicious soul once told me). In any event, I have firmly resolved, when and if the time should come, to wear my own naked scalp proudly and undisguised. I've also decided to collect hats from around the world.

There are, of course, a thousand other shocks that mortal—and male—flesh is heir to. Everything from falling pectorals to falling arches, from sagging shoulders to knobby knees. The whole discouraging catalogue was on display last summer when I went to Jones Beach for the day with my friend Ralph. Now Ralph might be said to have a bit of the endomorph about him, while I lean decidedly toward the ecto side. So between us, there wasn't a single, older male specimen on the beach that one of us didn't draw some grim conclusion from. Ralph saw himself, 20 years hence, in the fat man in the straw hat, squashing a beach chair into the sand. I felt a special shudder of identification when a creaky old geezer scuttled by like a crab, wearing baggy bermuda shorts and an "I Love Aruba" T-shirt. (My innate good taste, I prayed, would at least survive the years unscathed.) But it did strike me as odd, after indulging in this depressing pastime for close to an hour, that we'd failed to notice the three, comely young women who'd set up camp not ten feet away.

"Don't you think this is a little strange," I said, "that for the past hour we've been watching all the old men go by instead of the young women? What's happened to us?"

"I don't know," said Ralph, "but let's change the subject, okay? Live for today. Eat, drink, and be merry. I brought some beer—want one?"

"Sure," I said.

With one hand, he flipped the top off the cooler, and with the other reached in, rummaged around, and pulled out two cold, wet cans. Of Miller Lite.

____How to Pick Up a Man_

Last month, as part of some article research I was doing, I attended one of those adult-education, night classes. Of course, I wouldn't be totally honest with you if I said I went strictly in the line of duty. For years I'd heard that night courses were a great way to meet people, particularly other people also on the lookout. So before I left the house, I put on my new blue sport jacket, old underwear (see page 3) and a light splash of Aramis 900 Herbal After Shave. I also tucked some newly-printed business cards into my jacket pocket, where I could quickly get at them when a crowd of ardent women started clamoring for my phone number. I always like to be prepared for an emergency.

And for a minute or two, I actually thought there might be one. I had no sooner unfolded a metal chair and sat down in the classroom than I noticed a small, red-haired woman lingering in the doorway and looking my way. To my amazement, she grabbed a chair and began navigating her way across the room directly toward me.

"Well, what do you know?" I thought. "Someone's really gonna try to pick me up! Why didn't I buy this new jacket sooner?"

Setting up her chair right next to mine, she plunked herself down, and with one hand purposefully extended, said, "Hi, I'm Annabelle."

"Hi, I'm Robert," I wittily replied.

"What do you do?" she asked.

When I told her, she said, "Oh, I'd like to write articles and things, too. What's your phone number? I'll give you a call."

Fumbling for one of my cards, I handed it over, she tossed it into her purse (without even noticing the handsome embossing job) and after providing a handful of perfunctory details about herself, she suddenly claimed to recognize another man sitting toward the back of the room and excused herself. By the time the class break rolled around, she was sitting next to a third guy. (Or maybe it was her fourth—I think I lost count.) Nor did I ever hear from her again.

But still, I have to give credit where it is due. Annabelle had *chutzpah;* I haven't collected that many phone numbers in the past six years. It's a nerve-wracking job approaching a perfect stranger, and Annabelle had displayed exemplary courage. Into that fearsome valley of rejection, into those jaws of potential indifference, she had boldly charged, time and time again. It's just too bad that she had made her sallies with so little finesse and grace; it's as if she had just taken a course in "Picking Up Men" (I later combed through the course catalogue and sure enough, there it was—"How to Meet Men in New York") and was now practicing her new techniques and gambits. I guess in a way I was her final exam. For guts, I give her an A; for form, a C.

Some of the mistakes that Annabelle was making were the same mistakes that men have been making, to the chagrin of women everywhere, for centuries. The art of picking someone up is an ancient and difficult one, requiring years of practice and experience before mastery can be achieved. Women are still fairly new to it, and need time yet to hone their skills, polish their opening lines, and perfect their approaches. I haven't a doubt in my mind that, given that time, they'll raise the art to levels of tact and intelligence it has never before seen. But in the meanwhile, in the modest hope of nudging things along a bit, I'd like to offer the following guidelines and suggestions. Who knows—someone may use them successfully on *me* someday.

The Overture

For years, men have been taking basically two approaches to the opening line. One group has been content to use the age-old formulas, the ever popular "Don't I know you from somewhere?", the blatantly calculating "Excuse me, but you must be a professional model" or the strikingly stupid but durable "Nice day if it don't rain." The other group, whose SATs are generally somewhat higher, believes instead that an opening line must be shockingly original in some way, a rare concoction of wit and whimsy that Noel Coward would have been proud to utter. These guys will labor for days over what they hope will prove to be *the* winning formula, that magically incantatory collection of words that will at once amuse, enrapture, and intrigue whomever they've approached.

Both groups, I think, miss the mark. The first because their lines are so trite and worn that just hearing them would put anyone to sleep ("Come here often?" "Not anymore."), the second because their come-ons so clearly display the arduous work that went into making them. Who wants to know somebody who's been hammering away at his opener for the past two weeks?

With opening lines, it's important to remember that no matter how gussied up they are, no matter how cleverly phrased, beautifully articulated, or cunningly disguised, they're still recognizable, from distances as great as 30 miles, as just that—opening lines. You can dress 'em up any which way you like—their intent is still clear.

That's why simplicity, I think, is always the best strategy. The minute you've thrown the pitch, the pitchee will know it. So don't make it a curve ball that will leave him speechless, confused, or uncomfortable. Throw him something with enough on it to hit back, but not so much that he'll miss the ball completely.

A good, practical opener carries within it a kernel of conversation. Something as simple as "This is the loudest party I've been to in years—I'm glad I don't live downstairs," at least gives him something to react to (provided he can be heard) and a subject—parties—to talk about. At a museum or art gallery, it's a cinch. You just wind up standing in front of the same painting for a moment, and make a respectably intelligent comment on it. (*Not* "I think the artist's delicate use of chiaroscuro owes much to the school of Caravaggio, don't you?" Keep it *simple*. Like "Isn't this a wonderful portrait—the expression on her face is so interesting." Let *him* then make some observation about the expression. If he mutters "Looks like she's on the rag, if you ask me," you'll probably want to move right along to the next picture—and guy.)

Another nice thing about parties, art galleries, or even a city park on a summer afternoon, is that they provide such innocuous settings for a pick-up. In a singles bar or discotheque, you're presumed to be on the make, guilty until proven innocent. You've also got to compete with flashing strobe lights, six-foot speakers, and hordes of other people just to make yourself seen and heard. That doesn't happen on a park bench, or at a watercolor exhibition. It's a simple, straightforward one-on-one—unnerving perhaps, but effective nonetheless.

Finally, if you do find yourself at a loud, wild party, you can always saunter up to a guy and ask him if he'd like to dance. Many men I've spoken to have volunteered that they find such an invitation easy, acceptable, and very often kind of sexy.

"I love it when a girl asks me to dance," one man said. "It's so easy to just take it from there, to start talking and all that after you've boogied together for a while."

Another one told me, quite unprompted, that "it's a huge turn-on. It gives you this great chance to see and feel each other move, before you even get to know each other. I can always tell, just from the way she dances, whether I'm going to like a girl or not."

But what if you should invite and he should refuse? Well, this *can* happen—some men are swine, some men are snooty, and some men, of which I count myself one, are just hopelessly, congenitally, *pathologically* incapable of dancing. When someone does ask me, which happens with the frequency of a full lunar eclipse, I am instantly confronted with a painful dilemma: I can either embarrass her slightly by declining on the spot, or I can truly mortify her by accepting. Once on the dance floor (through excessive drink, irrational high spirits, or a potent combination thereof), I move with all the fluid grace of a garbage truck stuck in third gear; twice, my partners have required post-dance hospitalization (on an out-patient basis). Spectators, suddenly feeling unwell, have been known to rush from the room. I mention this only so you'll know that there are some of us out there who, while declining the dance, do appreciate the invitation, and would be only too glad to sit down and talk instead. That much we know how to do.

The Follow-Through

Assuming that your opening line has gone over reasonably well, without that resounding thud we all so dread, you should be aware that you have cleared only the first hurdle, and a second one, even higher, now awaits. You have successfully outflanked the Cerberus who guards the gates, but you must now confront the monster who lurks within—a monster of your own making.

Is there any beast so ravenous and all-consuming, so great in size and unpredictable in conduct, as the awakened male ego? Any dragon as ancient, any giant as omnipotent? Even in this day and age, when women are fully entitled to approach men, it still isn't done so often that a man doesn't immediately inflate to three times his normal dimensions when he discovers himself "hit upon." Suddenly, he feels for an instant what Warren Beatty must feel like all the time. Adrenaline courses through his veins, pectorals expand beneath his shirtfront, his head is filled with pealing bells, blaring trumpets, and celestial choirs singing hymns of self-praise and congratulation. The din is unbelievable.

So you must understand that it will take at least a few minutes before he can really hear what you've gone on to say. Go slow; wait until the hallelujahs have begun to fade, and his rump has returned to the bar stool. Even then, take care that you don't come on *too* aggressively. Now that you've taken the initiative and broken the ice, he will probably want to flex his muscles a bit, and show that he, too, can be assertive and in charge. I'm not saying that you should slip meekly into the backseat now; I'm merely suggesting that you let him share the front with you.

Men can act mighty skittish when being picked up. They're flattered and pleased to have been approached, but unless they can feel some semblance of control again, they're liable to start entertaining some foolish, but destructive, thoughts. If they start to feel corralled, they'll rear up on you like a wild stallion. "Boy, is she desperate," they'll think. "There must really be something wrong with her." Or, "What a man-eater—she probably goes through a different guy every week." What in fact are their own problems they'll fob off on you; their own fears and insecurities they'll translate into *your* desperation, or nymphomania. And despite all the jokes to the contrary, few and far between are the men who would actually want an insatiable woman—what men want is a woman they *can* satisfy.

I might add that the old tactic of "working the room," as practiced by our good friend Annabelle, is as offensive to men as it is to women when they're on the receiving end. Nobody minds being politely approached—it's nice to feel that you've effortlessly projected some magnetic appeal to another person—but to discover a short while later that you've been just another minor objective in a major mopping-up operation, its not only deflating but downright annoying. Who among us likes to think of him or herself as just another scribble on a crumpled cocktail napkin, or but one of a thousand wriggling fish caught in a widely-thrown net? Or, to inject a personal note, as just one more business card (beautifully embossed, to boot) tossed to the bottom of a bottomless purse? No one does. So even if you have embarked on a major big-game safari, keep it to yourself—don't make it apparent to all the quarry in a ten-mile radius by beating every bush in sight. Unless the man you've approached either (a) doesn't speak the language, or (b) speaks it obnoxiously, spend a humane amount of time with him before posting off to the hunt again.

Breaking off a conversation that is fast going nowhere is, to my mind, the hardest part of the whole pick-up procedure. Sometimes all it takes is 30 seconds before you know this is not going to work out—you ask him if he's in town on business, and he says no, on parole. You compliment a guy on his unusual necktie, and he says thanks, it's the official club tie of the American Fascists Society. Would you be interested in some literature? How do you beat a hasty, but courteous, retreat? (After all, you don't know what that first guy went to jail for.) Pretending to recognize someone, preferably someone way across the room, is one method; Annabelle, you may recall, favored this one. Suddenly remembering an appointment, after a quick glance at your watch, is another—but as this method requires that you leave the get-together altogether in order to be convincing, it's more of a last resort really. Simpler by far, at a party or bar, is to be sure the drink you've been idly swirling in your hand is down to its last ice cube and almost gone—with a single quick swallow, you can always drain the glass and excuse yourself to go and get it refreshed. If he decides, unbidden, to come along, you may elect to make a sudden detour to the bathroom. Depending on how awful he is, you may elect to spend anywhere from five minutes to a long weekend in there, waiting him out. Some women carry paperbacks with them wherever they go for just such emergencies.

Clinching the Deal

But let us imagine, if only for argument's sake, that the man you've met is not a recently released convict, or still in mourning for the passing of the Third Reich. Let us imagine that he's a nice, normal guy, with whom you've just enjoyed a nice, normal conversation. The time comes when, to borrow a phrase from the salesman's argot, you must "ask for the order." If you'd like to see him again sometime, or at least let him know that you would, you've got to do something to ensure that you know how to find each other. Vital information—such as last names and phone numbers—must change hands.

Sometimes, this rather sticky business can be circumvented altogether—if, in the course of the conversation, you've gotten his full name and he's mentioned that he works at the law firm of Squeezeplay and Grabbit, you're home free. You know how to reach him.

But what if he hasn't conveyed these precious stats? And what if, even after you've pointedly mentioned that you've got to be running very soon, he still hasn't summoned up the nerve, or resolve, to ask for *your* number? Well, you can either abandon the case on grounds of insufficient interest, or you can come right out and ask him for his. I say this lightly, but I *know,* I've been there, how hard this can be.

That's why I recommend, stodgy as it may seem, that you carry a business card. Instead of scrounging around in the dim recesses of your purse for a pen (no doubt dry) and a scrap of paper (an old grocery receipt), how much smoother, more professional and poised it is to offer your card, crisp, white, and bearing all the salient information. In one simple move, you have not only signaled an end to this encounter, but a desire to enjoy another one at some point in the future. Unless the guy is extraordinarily rude, uninterested, or just out of cards (which he surely will tell you) he'll reflexively offer you one of his own in return.

What do you say as, your heart pounding and your face flushing, you oh so casually extend this card? Well, one thing I can advise is *not* to do as I do: Do not attempt to conceal your embarrassment or tension behind an ever-thickening cloud of mindless babble. A better idea is, as always, to remain simple and direct. "I've really enjoyed talking to you. Maybe we could have lunch sometime." An invitation to lunch, or a suggestion that you meet for drinks, is so harmless and unpresumptuous that even the most fainthearted of us can, with practice, learn to utter it without undue stammering or confusion. And unlike a full-scale, Saturday night date, these occasions are so easily circumscribed that if, after an hour or so, they're not going as well as you'd hoped, you can always claim you have to race back to the office, or plead a dinner date for later that night (with your steady boyfriend, who's just returned from an assignment in Uruguay).

There may even be times, *mirabile dictu,* when you won't have to make such excuses. Sometimes, for no apparent reason, a benevolent god chooses to smile down upon you, and before you know it, you find yourself laughing, talking, truly enjoying yourself. Before you know it, drinks have naturally, seamlessly, segued into dinner, dinner into dancing, dancing into a nightcap, a nightcap into three handsome children, a Golden Retriever, and a lovely clapboard house on a leafy country lane. All these things can indeed come to pass, this mighty oak indeed can grow, from an acorn as tiny and insignicant as "Nice party, don't you think?"

___A Few Words About... the One-Night Stand___

After all I've just said, I wonder in how many minds the thought is revolving, "What planet is this guy from? What does he think pick-ups are all about? Hasn't he ever heard of sex?"

Just to set the record straight, yes, I have. So far, what I've heard has been confusing and contradictory, but I hope soon to get it all sorted out.

In the meantime, yes, I really do realize that sometimes, when the moon is full, when a warm summer breeze blows through the air, when you glance in the mirror and think "Geez, do I look great tonight!" a young woman's fancy, just like any man's, can turn to thoughts of love—or lust. Delightful as it is when those two go together, there are also times when they don't. Randiness can strike, without warning or provocation, like a swarm of mosquitoes, and leave you just as conscious of your own skin. Indeed, I have experienced the peculiar itch myself.

Today, we are in more of a position to scratch than we have ever been before. I won't go so far as to claim that one-night stands and casual sex are strictly twentieth-century American inventions, but I will say that I find it hard to imagine a cultural milieu where sex is more openly accepted, more routinely indulged in, and easily available than it is right here, right now. And I'm not complaining. All in all, I think that's a good thing—sex *should* be governed by our own individual needs and our individual desires; public institutions, like legislatures and churches, ought, for the most part, to stay out of it. But lately, I've occasionally caught myself wondering if, while freeing ourselves sexually, we haven't managed to constrain ourselves emotionally, if in fact we haven't made a sort of bargain with the Devil—which, like most such bargains, we can't fail to lose in the end.

Last Saturday night, for example, at a party—where else?—I happened to meet a woman I'd met briefly once before, at yet another party. This time we picked up where we'd left off, and to make a short story even shorter, ended up spending the night together at my apartment. The next morning I awoke at eight A.M. to the aroma of freshly brewed coffee—which I never drink before ten, when I normally rise—and to the sound of the local "Easy Listening" station, which I listen to only when gagged and bound. My guest's name was Elizabeth, but I wasn't sure if she liked to be called Liz, Betsy, or Beth. She took a shot on "Rob" for me, though that turns out to be the only variant of my name I've never really used. (Rather than embarrass us both, I adopted it for the day.)

Later on, on our way to brunch, I casually tried to take her hand, but wound up with a gaggle of knuckles and fingertips instead. When she attempted to slip her arm through mine, she discovered that we were completely out of step. Nor was she aware—how could she be?—that all my life I've been incapable of speaking to anyone walking on my left side; I can only talk to the right.

It's such an odd sensation really, knowing so much about a person in one way—where she's ticklish, how she sleeps, what gives her physical pleasure—and so very little about her in every other way. What did Elizabeth—Liz?—want to do with her life, what did she worry about, how did she spend her evenings at home? Did she subscribe to the opera, or hang out at the punk clubs? Was she a member of the Audubon Society, or a litterbug? How did she feel about nuclear power, video games, the melting of the polar ice caps? And how on earth do you ask somebody about all these things at once?

Becoming close to someone is a complicated process even under ideal circumstances—but after you've already slept together, the whole procedure seems to be so oddly skewed; it feels so backwards and so artificial somehow, asking how many brothers or sisters you each have when you already know such intimate details about the other. The stakes have been raised so high, so fast, that all the commonplace conversation that real intimacy is built on sounds false, forced, perfunctory. In one night, you may already have learned too much, too soon—without knowing each other well enough to understand, nor caring enough to sympathize, you may pass too harsh and summary a judgment on the other; sudden, "unearned" intimacy may wind up precluding any chance of the real thing turning up later.

I'm reminded of an incident from my first year in New York, when I shared an office with a guy named Paul. Since our wages, adjusted for time and place, were roughly what the Pharaohs paid for pyramid work, we were forced to resort to all sorts of money-saving stratagems—one was to drink the office coffee, a vile-smelling, jet-black fluid that anyone in funds would have shuddered to contemplate. Another was to finish the day at a bar off Sixth Avenue that served an especially lavish assortment of hors d'oeuvres as part of its "Happy Hour" buffet. For the price of one domestic beer, carefully nursed, we could plow our way through plateloads of tiny wieners and fried chicken wings.

Paul, however, had another reason for frequenting the place; he had developed an enormous crush on the bartender, a lithesome brunette attired every night in a starched white shirt and tight black trousers. Most of the time, she took no notice of us, other than to draw our beers and take our money, but on one lucky Wednesday, Paul actually managed to break through her cool veneer and engage her in conversation. Happy for my friend, but clearly superfluous, I gulped down three or four Swedish meatballs, clapped him on the back (he didn't seem to notice), and pushed off. On the bus, I regretted not having packed some chicken wings in a napkin for the slow trip home.

Next morning, as I sipped from my bitter cup, Paul scrambled into the office half an hour late, his hair a mess, his tie untied, and all his clothes suspiciously familiar.

"Have I ever mentioned how much I love that outfit?" I said, swiveling in my chair. "Loved it yesterday, love it even more today."

Paul tossed his rumpled sportcoat onto the hatrack in the corner. "Is there any of that rancid coffee left?"

"Of course—nobody drinks it but you and me."

When he'd returned, gingerly holding his hot styrofoam cup, I demonstrated my maturity by not asking what happened for fully 15 seconds. In fact, it was Paul who first broached the subject.

"Dying to know, aren't you?"

"Not dying—let's just say curious."

"Well," he said, sipping the coffee and grimacing, "we talked at the bar until eight, when she went off duty, then I walked her back to her place, about 20 blocks uptown, where we talked some more. We even watched a TV movie-of-the-week together. One thing led to another," he said, with a surprising lack of enthusiasm, "and, well, here I am today, wearing yesterday's clothes."

"Pardon me for saying so, but wasn't this the girl of your dreams? You've been going on about her for the past two months, and now you describe the whole experience as if you were reciting the stock tables in the business section."

Staring down into his cup, he said, "I'm just trying to let

you down easy. I'm just trying to find a way to say that her apartment was a pig sty, her legs and armpits have never been shaved, and she snores worse than my father." He glanced up at me, and I could see that his heart wasn't really up to the jesting. "I suggest we find a new 'Happy Hour' place."

He remained, for the rest of the day, less than his usual buoyant self. We kidded around a bit, just for form's sake, about his "night of passion," but it was clear that he was really disillusioned, even depressed, over it. For months, he'd been fantasizing about this woman, but now that he'd actually spent a night with her, he was crushed. What he'd finally learned about her hadn't at all jibed with his expectations; what was real had put a brutal stop to what he'd been imagining. Her legs were unshaven, she snored in her sleep—in someone we care for, these are not major problems. In someone we don't know, someone we're acquainted with in only a one-dimensional way, they can be—anything at all that turns off the sexual current turns off everything else, too. Precisely because there *is* nothing else.

In a way, it's a little like the experience of going to a porn film—what we're watching is graphic, uncensored, no-holds-barred, and boring. We don't know who these people on the screen are, we don't care, and neither, it seems, do they. In fact, it's worse than boring—the grapplings are so impersonal, joyless, and rapid-fire, that you leave the theater inexorably drawn to the monastic orders.

In direct contrast, consider a movie like *Coming Home,* in which the love scenes between Jon Voight and Jane Fonda were, if you ask me, genuinely erotic and exciting. Why? Because the characters they played, the paraplegic Vietnam vet and the gallant wife of an officer still serving there, became real people for us. We saw them gradually come to know and care for each other, we saw the sex between them as a natural, even inevitable culmination of who they were and how they felt. If we wantonly lopped off the first half of that movie, those characters would no longer be able to engage us at all, and their sex scenes would look empty and staged. It just seems to me that if we do the same thing in our own lives, lop off all the early stuff, what we get in the end is sure to be just as mechanical and just as meaningless. If we don't allow desire to build up, then how in the world, I wonder, can we ever expect passion to explode?

Part II

Whatever Happened to Dating, Anyway?

In Praise of Ancient Customs____

For four years, I went out with—in fact, I was virtually married to—one woman. On the night we finally decided to break it off, due to insurmountable and irreconcilable differences (she lived in New Jersey, I lived in New York, and we both refused to budge), I walked out to Second Avenue with her to hail a cab. I opened the door for her, then leaned in for a brief but poignant parting kiss. As I drew back, with a look of unspeakable tragedy in my eyes, a sudden gust of wind picked up an empty Kentucky Fried Chicken bag and flattened it smoothly across my face. I should have known it was a kind of omen.

But unfortunately, I wasn't that astute. Instead, I found myself anticipating, with some relish, the life of that ever-popular figure of American lore, the "swinging bachelor." And here in New York, no less, that much-vaunted den of iniquity. After four years of unsullied fidelity, I was at last free to sow my oats again, to cut my swath, to "score" (assuming such an expression was still used) like mad. When I met a woman, I could lie through my teeth about what I did for a living, I could speak with an English accent if I thought it would help, I could stay out as late as I liked without calling in. Best of all, I'd say to myself (chiefly in those moments of heartsick despair), I could unpack and polish up those formidable "dating" skills I'd acquired through a long and arduous apprenticeship at Evanston High. I could charm her with my witty badinage, impress her with my keen sensitivity to women writers, surprise her with a gentle kiss on her closed eyelids.

To be perfectly honest, I rather looked forward to the stately progression of affection that I imagined a new affair would offer, to the hand-holding and tentative kisses, the impulsive gifts and frequent phone calls (for cooked-up reasons), to all of what Aldous Huxley once described as "the chaste pleasures and sublimated sensualities more thrillingly voluptuous than any of the grosser deliriums." (Which is not to say those "grosser deliriums" didn't cross my mind, too, on occasion—I _am_ only human.) But how was I to know, in my unworldly innocence, that my ideas of dating were as out-of-date as the Dave Clark Five? That I was entering into a brave new world where the only reason for candlelight was a power outage, where the traditional male prerogatives had been usurped or abandoned, and where the courtly mating ritual had been compressed to the length of a station break? I ask you, how could I have known all that?

What I had in mind was a nice, pleasant evening out— dinner in some reasonably charming bistro (classy enough to provide tablecloths, modest enough to dispense with captains and wine stewards) and then perhaps an Off-Broadway show, a movie, or a nightclub featuring a cover charge within easy grasp of your basic, freelance writer. At the end of such diverse entertainments, I imagined myself escorting my companion home, perhaps kissing her goodnight after she'd fumbled for her keys, then returning to my comfy rocking chair to make some inroads into the Sunday *New York Times*. It wasn't long before I was disabused of my hopelessly old-fashioned notions.

A matchmaking friend, Sally, set me up with a friend of hers named Connie. On Friday night, Connie and I went to dinner at an Italian restaurant, then to a jazz club to listen to some music, then back to her place (see how well I stick to my game plan) where she invited me in for a drink. After the drink, I kissed her goodnight and went home.

Sunday morning I got the call from Sally: "Sorry you didn't like Connie."

"I did like Connie. What makes you say that?"

"Connie does—she told me what happened."

"What happened? Nothing happened."

"Exactly."

"Huh?"

"She invited you in for a drink."

"And I had a drink."

"And then you left."

In the long accusatory silence that followed, I not only got the message, but, I must confess, a certain amount of ego gratification. I was a hit as a bachelor, I hadn't lost my touch! But a moment later, I was dumbfounded. Had Connie expected me to come on, on our first date? Had I missed some overt invitation? Were there some universally understood code-words that I alone didn't know? Had I committed some unpardonable offense simply by minding my manners?

Further rumination left me even more puzzled. Connie, I was convinced, had had no more real desire for a passionate encounter that night than I did. Magnificent as I'll admit I can sometimes be, still I am *not* irresistible (please, no arguments). Nor am I blind. Connie and I had enjoyed a perfectly nice evening together, but if fireworks had been going off, I don't think I'd have missed them. So what on earth, I wondered, was going on here?

A few more weeks on the dating scene, asking out various women simply for the pleasure of their company rather than from any insatiable, uncontrollable desire, and I began to notice an odd trend emerging. Before a date, *I* was the one who was starting to worry about how the evening was going to end, about whether I was leading her on in any way, about how I would deal with a direct or an indirect sexual overture. I was suddenly dealing with what had been, for time immemorial, a woman's problems—and problems even she wasn't supposed to have had to worry about this early on in the game! Before the most routine dinner date, I was wondering about whether the evening would end with a chaste goodnight kiss or passionless groping, with an honest smile or a dishonest avowal of undying affection. The simple, time-honored "date," I discovered, had suddenly become a moral dilemma and a major production. Why?

Much as I hate to have to advert to anything called "the sexual revolution," I'm afraid there's just no way around it. Not so long ago, it bumped off some sitting ducks like virginity and the double standard (how successfully remains to be seen), but one of the less noticed casualties seems to have been dating. The old boy-meets-girl, boy-gets-to-know-girl, boy-and-girl-fall-in-love scenario appears to have gone in for radical surgery, and emerged in a drastically foreshortened state; five minutes after they meet these days, the question in the air is not whether the boy and girl will grow to like each other but which side of the bed each will prefer.

Traditionally, women have been the put-upon ones. They're the ones who've had to toe that fine line between being encouraging and being a "tease," who've had to gauge how far they could go without stepping beyond what a "nice girl" should do—that ancient "but will you respect me in the morning" dilemma. The last ten years have changed most of that—as one woman told me, "I feel that I can go out with a guy three times now—tops—before I'm expected to sleep with him, or stop accepting his invitations altogether. Most of the time," she adds, "it's not a problem—if I haven't come around by the second date, I don't hear from him again."

Another woman I know, a book publicist, told me about attending a big publishing bash where she met a prominent editor. "We had a great time at the party, and he introduced me to zillions of people I'd never have met on my own. He asked me if I'd like to get together sometime, and I said sure. I was praying I hadn't said it too quickly. Anyway, he called me a couple of days later, asked if I was free for the coming weekend, and then announced that he'd booked us a room at a resort hotel in Montauk. He was already telling me what to pack and wear, before I was able to blurt out something brilliant like, 'Wait a second—we're supposed to go away for the weekend together? We haven't even gone out yet!' He seemed to be *amazed* that I was so old-fashioned about all this—and the weird thing was, *I* felt a little like some kind of prude, too. He eventually apologized for jumping to conclusions, and swore up and down that he'd call me again when he got back from the island, but of course he never did. I spent the whole weekend eating rum raisin Häagen-Dazs and alternating between feeling infuriated, and feeling like a fool."

Faced with such predicaments increasingly often, a lot of women do wind up going against their own better judgment or inclinations. They sleep with a guy because if they don't, they envision an endless succession of lonely, rum raisin weekends. To wait, they fear, is to jeopardize any chance whatsoever of finding a real relationship. They hedge their bets by going to bed—which is exactly what Connie had in mind, I suspect. But when I didn't even attempt to seduce her that night, I guess she figured it was a lost cause, that I just wasn't interested in pursuing things at all. (She was, incidentally, wrong.)

But men, you might think, have finally gotten exactly what *they've* always wanted—the female population, or at least a large part of it, cowed into submission and acquiescence, and all, conveniently, in the name of "liberation." Maybe some men *are* happy about that; it's just that I don't know them.

The men I know are starting to feel the pressure to "put out" (as it has been so inelegantly phrased) and "to perform" that women have had to put up with for so long. If a woman expects me to make certain demands of her on a date, then those expectations weigh on me in turn; if I don't forge ahead sexually, she may be relieved, she may be disappointed, and she may—and this is the most surprising reaction of all—be a little insulted. Even if she had no intention of going to bed with me, she may be a trifle miffed that I didn't think enough of her even to make the attempt. And so, just to reestablish the natural order of things, I sometimes give it the old college try—and take my rebuke quite gracefully.

But what a pass have we come to then, that women should find themselves feigning passion to keep a man from absconding, and men should find themselves feigning passion to keep the woman from questioning their virility—or worse, their basic sexual orientation. Is anybody having any fun here anymore?

Judging from what I read about the rise of impotence among young American males—and from what I'm told by women about their own ambivalence, anger, and confusion—sometimes it seems doubtful. Our famous modern technology can fly us to Paris in less than three hours, or cook our dinner in under three minutes, but unfortunately it can't do a damn thing to hurry along human relationships. They take as long to grow today as they ever did. As far as I'm concerned, that's fine—my fondest memories are not of one-night stands but of prolonged romances; my greatest "conquest" was not an elaborate seduction but a simple, declarative kiss on a sofa in Michigan. Among all my friends and acquaintances, I can't think of a single, solid working relationship that couldn't have survived a couple of weeks, even months, of good, old-fashioned dating at its inception—but I can think of plenty of *bad* ones that wouldn't have stood the test. Dating, I am well aware, is a word that smacks of high school and varsity letter sweaters, but it's a pity, I think, if it's left at that. In my own humble opinion, dating and all of its attendant glories—hand-holding, kissing, flowers, and phone calls, even the occasional case of nerves—ought to be fully reinstated in the adult lexicon.

Only this time around, I'm quite willing to concede, we can do without that 11:30 curfew.

____Are Looks All That Matter to Men?____

"You know the funny thing about Bo Derek? I mean, she's got an unbelievable body, it's one of the wonders of the world, but she just doesn't do anything for me. She just doesn't get my *juices* going."

"Me, neither," agreed Sam. "I guess that's why I broke up with her. Anybody want another beer?" He fished around in the cooler, and pulled out a dripping can of Coors.

There were four of us, sprawled around on the grass of the Sheep Meadow in Central Park. We'd just finished a strenuous game of Frisbee football, and had now retired to the shade of a large tree—oak, elm, I never could tell one from another—for our usual intellectual discourse and debate.

"The problem with Bo," Larry continued, in his finest Aristotelian manner, "is that she *is* the perfect ten—everything is exactly what and where it's supposed to be. The blonde hair, the blue eyes, the knockers that could—"

"Please," Sam interrupted, looking hurt, "show some consideration. I'm still not entirely over her."

"Knockers that could stop a truck. There's no room for improvement there, no room for imagination."

"I think there is," said Mike. "I think she's in dire need of a personality transplant; talk about nobody being home. You wanna know who's *really* sensational? I'll tell you who's really sensational—Jacqueline Bissett."

At the mention of this name, my own heart skipped a beat.

"Okay, so she's been in some of the worst movies ever made—it's not *her* fault if she can't get a decent part. The great thing about Bissett is that she's not only gorgeous, she looks—and is—intelligent, too. I saw her do an interview once with Cavett."

"Did she mention my name?" Sam asked, sipping from his Coors.

"Yes, Bissett's not bad," Larry concurred, with great deliberation. "But as far as I'm concerned, there's nobody around today who can even remotely compare with Lauren Bacall, in the days when she was making movies like 'To Have and Have Not.' Remember, that great scene when she tells Bogart that if he wants her, he should just whistle: 'You know how to whistle, don't you? You just put your lips together, like this, and blow.' I remember seeing that movie for the first time when I was about 12 years old, on the Early Show, and even though I wasn't sure exactly what that line was all about, I knew that if I went to my mother and asked her, she'd take away my TV privileges for the rest of my life."

Off and on, over the next hour or so, while we continued to discuss everything from the Hegelian dialectic to the disintegration of East-West détente, one of us would throw another name into the hopper—Mike volunteered that if he couldn't have Jackie Bissett, he'd settle for Julie Christie; Larry championed Katharine Hepburn ("as she was when she made *Philadelphia Story*"), Ingrid Bergman ("in *Casablanca*, of course"), and a newcomer named Rachel Ward ("I predict great things for her"); Sam, true to form, wistfully adverted to his affairs with all of them; and I, not wanting to let the gang down, suggested Peggy Fleming, Hayley Mills, on whom I developed a lasting crush when my mother drove me to the Valencia Theatre, on my seventh birthday, to see *Pollyanna*, and, of course, Ms. Bissett (to whom I would also like to now dedicate this book).

Even more interesting than the names that did come up, however, were the names that didn't—all the poster queens and TV starlets, the media hypes of the immediate moment, whose stars begin to fade almost as soon as they are sighted, whose accomplishments and appeal—like Ms. Derek's—can be instantly computed by anyone in possession of a tape measure. When it came right down to the true contenders for our hearts' top honors, we had all dismissed out of hand the centerfolds and swollen glands, and chosen instead a far more eclectic and interesting batch of women. Yes, they were all attractive—after all, if you're fantasizing, why not?—but they were also complex, intelligent, truly talented, even sometimes mysterious, individuals. Given the frivolous nature of the conversation, I think we'd acquitted ourselves pretty well.

Surprising as it may seem, I believe that most other men would, too. Oh, sure, we may buy the occasional issue of *Playboy*, our heads may turn when a skimpy bikini passes us on the beach, but that is only evidence of how easily our attention can be captured. Briefly. Our lasting passions, our serious predilections, are more difficult to describe, harder to fathom, and impossible to guess.

I remember, for instance, the surprise with which I received a letter one day from a guy I'd known for ages. For

Lord knows what reason, and in what romantic fervor, he had decided to record for posterity, and mail to me, what he considered to be his "Ideal Woman." Who needs to read any further, I thought, after seeing that title, all in caps, emblazoned across the top of the page? I know what Karl's ideal woman is—she's one of those department store mannequins, prettily chiseled, long-legged, hugely stacked, and thoroughly lobotomized, that he's been going out with all his life. She's one of those flashy ornaments that he's felt compelled, for as long as I've known him, to wear on his arm. Who needs to read?

But as we'd been friends for many years, and as I don't get that much mail, I did—and quickly discovered that I didn't know Karl even half as well as I'd smugly thought. The ideal woman he described, in thoughtful, scrupulous detail, was sensitive, loving, intelligent ("I know that may come as a shock to you, Robert, but it really does matter to me, more so everyday"), happy and successful at whatever profession she'd chosen (just so long as she wasn't an architect, as Karl was: "I'd like a little diversity in the relationship"), good-natured, garrulous ("sometimes, I'll admit, I need some help keeping up my end of a conversation"), slightly impractical ("I like to be in charge when it comes to planning things"). Throughout the letter, Karl displayed a self-awareness, a modesty, and a tact, that I had never before noticed in him. Even his prose style, something to which people in my line of work are especially attentive, was strong and fluent. The letter impressed me enormously.

As did its sentiments. Karl and I were in our late 20s now; we hadn't been in very close touch since our college years, but in a strange way we seem to have kept pace with each other. Much of what he expressed in his letter were things that I myself had come to want, anticipate, brood over. In our attitude toward women, in particular, we'd come from rather different directions, but appeared to have arrived, as if predestined to do so, at pretty much the same place. He might want a talkative woman, I might want a laconic one (I'm easily loud enough for any two people), but in the importance we placed on the essential qualities, in her value as an individual and her warmth as a companion, we were in perfect agreement.

When women ask what men want, as Freud was wont to do about women, it's impossible to formulate any sort of sensible reply. Which men? Barley farmers in the Carpathian foothills? Auto workers in Detroit? Dentists in Toledo? Even if the question is further refined—"What do English-speaking men, between the ages of 20 and 40, currently residing in the United States, and having no prior record of a felony arrest, look for in a woman they'd like to ask out?"—the question remains very nearly insoluble. All that can be observed and pointed out are certain trends and general tendencies, common to most, if never quite all, of the men in the formally delineated target group. But keeping all these disclaimers firmly in mind, and leaving room for as many more as needed to be added on later, there are, I believe, a few things that *can* be said about what truly matters to men.

Mostly, I think, it depends on how old they are—the men, that is. The very same man, at 18 and 28, will have substantially different priorities, as was the case with Karl. What once seemed paramount may wind up inconsequential; what was once entirely overlooked may, with the passage of a few years, loom large. That Beauty Factor in particular (as it is known among us social scientists) undergoes a sizable sea change.

Roughly from the moment of his conception, a male is brought up to value in a female, above almost all other attributes, Beauty. Winning the favors and attention of the prettiest girl in the class—by riding his bicycle the fastest, hitting three home runs in the Little League game, or setting off a firecracker in the cloakroom (my own modus operandi)—is an unmatchable coup, even at an age when the danger of "cooties" may prevent a boy from overtly demonstrating his affection for a girl in any other way short of physical abuse. My own great love for a girl named Gail, whose braided pigtails tied with bright red ribbons drove me wild with desire, was tortuously transmuted into a vigorous shove on the playground one day. When she fell on the asphalt and scraped her knees, I thought I would die with shame and anguish.

Rather than getting hopelessly entangled in the "nature vs. nurture" controversies, I'll simply concede, right up front, that a lot of the reason little boys are drawn to the pretty little girls, just as pretty little girls are drawn to the cute little boys, is no doubt purely instinctual; people just naturally admire well-spaced features, shiny hair, nicely colored eyes. But if that accounts for maybe half the attraction, surely the rest comes from all sorts of cultural pressures and inducements. Life is one great carnival booth, and walking off with the showiest Kewpie doll gets you lots of attention. (I believe it was Goethe who said that.)

The lesson was brought home to me, with lasting impact, around my sophomore year of high school when, as one of my early forays into dating, I asked out a girl named Martha, who was generally acknowledged to be the smartest person in the school. In addition to that, Martha was sweet, kind, considerate, good company—but she wasn't what you'd call a looker. I asked her out because I wanted to go out on a date, because I thought she was nice, and because I thought she'd accept my invitation—after all, I wasn't exactly the captain of the football team either. We had a pretty good time, too. Went to see an Italian movie with subtitles, then, in keeping with the flavor of the film, to a popular pizza joint. At her door, under the front porch light, I'd even managed to plant a quick kiss on her without missing her lips. The date had gone off with no major hitches, as far as I could tell, and I was very pleased with myself.

Until the following Monday, when I happened to mention it over lunch with some friends in the cafeteria. Nobody greeted the news with much enthusiasm, and I thought for an instant I'd even seen a couple of the guys exchange a look of some bemusement. One of them said, a little too idly, "Martha, huh—how come you asked her out?"

"I don't know—no special reason, I guess." I was already regretting having opened my mouth.

"I thought you had the hots for Tina." Tina was one of the cheerleaders.

"Well, sure, who doesn't—"

"Martha's in my trig class," another one interjected. "Man, what a slide rule that girl is."

"You know, I bet if you asked out Tina, she'd go. Why don't you give her a try?"

"That Martha, man—I don't know why she bothers taking classes, she oughta be teaching them. Say, did you guys hear that Hoster blew up the third-floor chem lab?"

Suddenly, the table erupted into laughter and talking, Hoster had screwed up again, what a card, how many times could they suspend him. I sat quietly, unwrapping my Twinkies, glad of the reprieve. My weekend victory had suddenly lost much of its luster—why *was* I going out with Martha? I mean, sure she was nice enough and all that, but maybe I should have been aiming higher. Maybe Tina *would* go out with me if I asked, maybe it wasn't so impossible. Even cheerleaders had to go out with somebody. By the time the cafeteria bell rang and we adjourned for the next period, I'd not only convinced myself that I might actually be Tina material, but that my date with Martha hadn't really been so great after all. During the week, I bumped into Martha in the halls a couple of times, but I didn't get around to asking her out again. And when, after a lot more prompting, I did ask Tina, she turned me down flat, thereby introducing me to what is known in literary circles as "poetic justice."

Mortified as I am at the recollection of this adolescent spinelessness, I offer it as a case in point, an example of the awful, little ways in which even the finest, the most noble and upstanding nature can be subtly corrupted and misdirected—so you can imagine how easy it was to muck up *mine*. Every day, in a myriad of indiscernible ways, a man is reminded that the woman he's seen with is a direct reflection of his own masculinity, of his status, his success, his power; she's seen by other men, and consequently by her own man too, as a medal on his chest, a feather in his cap, a living, breathing, walking, talking endorsement of his own worth and position in life. The prettier she is, the more he puffs out his chest feathers, the more he struts and crows. For a lot of men, this lesson, once learned, is never forgotten.

Those are the guys who go on to collect beautiful women like bowling trophies, who compulsively chase one after the other, who bounce like Ping-Pong balls from one to the next. They seldom want just one beautiful woman, they generally want them all. They're out to prove that they can do it, that they're irresistible, that no woman is beyond their grasp. The women themselves are incidental; once he's demonstrated that he can have them, once he's inveigled them into giving themselves to him, his interest rapidly subsides, and he's off in search of the next likely target. He imagines himself in some sort of contest with all other men, feverishly running in a race that he alone heard the starting pistol for, a race that has no finish line, that he can never hope to win.

Karl, my letter-writing friend, started out in just such a race, I think. But like most sensible men, men who grow up over the years and find other, more meaningful ways of validating themselves, he eventually discovered that women could be more than notches on the bedpost, or hunting trophies to mount on his wall. With that startling revelation there generally comes another one even more wonderful—women can be friends, companions, even, in some exceptional instances, soul-mates. If I harbored still the slightest doubt about the sincerity of Karl's conversion, it was effectively quashed last spring when I attended his wedding on Long Island.

The bride, I am delighted to announce, was not a knockout. She did not have waves of blonde hair cascading down her back, she did not have a 38-inch bust, she did not have Marlene Dietrich legs. She was short, a trifle on the plump side, and had belatedly decided to get braces to correct a slight overbite. So much for the debits.

On the credit side of the ledger, she had a law degree from Harvard, an incredibly warm and gregarious disposition (one of the qualities Karl had most desired, as you may recall), and, as she demonstrated at the rehearsal dinner, she could blow perfect smoke rings. I liked her a lot, and though I never thought I'd be able to do this, I congratulated Karl on his choice with genuine enthusiasm.

More and more, I find I'm able to do that these days. Most of the women my friends have recently married, moved in with, or gotten serious about, have been smart, likable, and, at least to my mind, a clear improvement over their earlier partners. Some of the women are beautiful, some of them aren't, but in either case, their physical attributes don't appear to have been the deciding factors in the relationships anymore. Other qualities, like compatibility, or commonality of interests, have been. In a totally cuckoo bit of inverse logic, which I nonetheless understand, my friend Ralph, the lawyer, even argues that as status symbols go, a plain woman is actually more valuable than a glamorous one: "You know what made that occur to me for the first time? When John Lennon married Yoko Ono. I mean, let's face it—she was an artist and an intellectual and all that, but she was not gorgeous. She was even older than he was. But here was John Lennon, my idol at the time, a man who could have virtually any woman he wanted, and that's who he had picked. It made me think that a man who's really secure, and confident in himself, who doesn't need any outside approval anymore, will pick a woman for more important reasons than her looks. And ever since then, I know this is weird, I've always suspected guys with really good-looking girls on their arms of being insecure, or maybe a little juvenile. I've even suspected *myself* when I've started to get involved with someone very good-looking—right away I start thinking extra-hard about it, like why am I really doing this? Do I really like this person, or am I just trying to convince myself that I do because I want to go to bed with her? I guess it's just one more way I've found of driving myself crazy."

Probably the most significant discovery most of my friends have lately made about Beauty, and I include myself in this group, is that it "lies in the eye of the beholder." Now how about that for a revelation? More pointedly, however, I think we've discovered that Beauty can also fluctuate, in the very same eye, as much as the most volatile stock on the stock exchange, that it can grow or dwindle just exactly as our affection grows or dwindles, that someone we thought beautiful one day can, after forfeiting our good opinion somehow, look much less appealing the very next time we meet.

It happened once to me over the course of a single meal. It was about a year after I'd graduated from college and moved to New York. For a few weeks, I'd been going out with a woman named Claire, who, and you'll just have to take my word for this, was truly, objectively, empirically, no-foolin' beautiful. Lustrous, auburn hair, slate-gray eyes flecked with green, a slender, understated figure. Trust me—she was beautiful.

And from the moment we were introduced, I was smitten. In no time, I was running all over town, arranging intimate dinners at restaurants I couldn't afford, reserving orchestra seats for Broadway shows, picking out romantic little gifts. In fact, I was so busy doing everything I could to impress and entertain her that I never stopped to notice along the way that, despite her beauty and blatant sensuality, Claire was imbued with all the wit and charm of your average cantaloupe.

The night it dawned on me, I had just returned from an overseas trip, and I was suffering from a serious case of jet lag. For once I was not my usual chatty self, rattling away at a mile a minute to keep the conversation rolling along. For once, I could only sit back, eat my dinner, and listen, really *listen,* to what Claire had to say. It was an enlightening experience.

She began with work, where she was being persecuted by everyone at the office. "It's just like that last job I had," she said, dabbling with her shrimp scampi. "My boss is always having a cow about something; to tell you the truth, I think I turn him on, and he can't take it, so he starts bitching. That's what happened at that last place, you know; that's the real reason they fired me."

Then went on to friends: "This girl I know, Marianne, she just got engaged to this guy who's really loaded. I mean, big bucks. She took me with her to his apartment once—what a place. White shag carpet, really deep, lots of that track lighting, a Jacuzzi in the bathtub. She won't ever have to do anything again—some people just have all the luck," she said, unwrapping a fresh pack of cigarettes.

Onward to entertainment: "Did you ever read that book *Worldly Goods*? You know, I just started reading it the other day, and it's okay, but I really think that if I had the time, and felt like doing it, I could easily have written it myself. I mean, it can't be all that hard to write a book like that. It's probably just who you know, knowing the right people who'll publish it. That's what everything always boils down to," she concluded, stubbing out her Virginia Slim in the ashtray.

Those were only some highlights. In nearly every story she told, envy or avarice figured strongly. Her thoughts were almost without exception petty, unfeeling, vindictive, or simply maniacally self-absorbed. She wasn't what you'd call a very nice person. And sitting there at the table, even in the thick of my transatlantic stupor, I could feel the scales finally falling from my eyes. I could see her at last, clearly, for who and what she was—and even her slate-gray eyes, flecked with green, suddenly seemed not nearly as striking as they once had. By the time the check arrived, I'd been forever cured of my infatuation with her.

But it took me years, slow learner that I am, to discover the flip-side of that Claire experience, to learn that just as Beauty can fade in someone you no longer care for, so can it grow in someone for whom you feel an ever-deepening regard. As the heart grows fonder, so does the eye. In a couple of instances that spring immediately to mind, I started out by dating perfectly ordinary-looking women, only to discover, some months and a wealth of affection later, that I was now walking arm-in-arm with a radiantly beautiful creature. The transformation was miraculous, and imperceptibly achieved. Love is without a doubt the subtlest make-over artist around, and at times when I've felt a little haggard or wan myself, I've relied upon it to touch me up, too, in my own sweetheart's eyes. So far, I think it's been doing a bang-up job.

The Phone Call: Men, Women, and Egos on the Line

The finger moves, hesitantly, toward the dial. It stops in mid-air, hovers, then suddenly withdraws. It taps on the desktop, nervously. Then moves forward again, this time it dials. One number. Two. Three. Four. Five. It pauses. Six. Another pause. Prolonged. The receiver is returned to the cradle. The finger taps out its desktop tattoo again.

A few minutes later, the receiver is hurriedly lifted, the finger lunges at the dial. 1-2-3-4-5-6-7, the numbers are dialed in rapid succession. The phone is ringing. Once, twice, three times.

"Hello?"

"Hi – there, – hope – I'm – not – catching – you – at – a – bad – time – right – now – if – I – am – I – can – call – back – later – I – hope – you – remember – me – we – met – at – the – regional – sales – conference – last – Thursday – some – lunch – they – served – us – huh – that – chicken – must – have – been – raised – in – a – rubber – factory – haha – I – was – seated – to – your – left – not – stage – left – just – left – haha – and – we – had – that – great – conversation – about – the – weather – and – I – was – just – wondering – if – you – were – maybe – free – sometime – I – thought – if – you – had – an – evening – to – spare – we – might – be – able – to – get – together – have – a – drink – or – dinner – or – something – there – are – about – a – zillion – movies – out – right – now – that – I'd – like – to – see – I'm – a – real – movie – buff – of – course – I – also – like – the – theater – and – if – there's – some – play – or – something – that – you'd – prefer – to – catch – instead – do – you – like – Chinese – food. . . ."

Is there anything at once so pitiable and so familiar as that phone call? Centuries ago, young bucks were probably sending up equally staccato smoke signals, inviting a maiden from the neighboring village to the summer solstice tribal dance. The only major change has been that women, too, can now make that call. They, too, can enjoy the nail-biting anxiety, the heart-stopping fear of rejection, the palm-sweating small talk that are all part and parcel of calling someone up for a date.

"I probably shouldn't admit this," says my friend Gerald, "but before I call someone up for the first time, I make up a little list of things I can say and talk about, and then put it right beside the phone. I'm deathly afraid of drawing a total blank. When the call's over, I tear the list into ten thousand pieces, set fire to it, then flush the ashes down the toilet. And I'm still worried somebody's gonna find it and expose me."

"Not my method at all," said Larry, when I told him how Gerald operated. "I find that if you have everything too laid-out and rehearsed, you're completely thrown for a loop as soon as the conversation departs from your prearranged script. I just believe in calling up and letting things happen— 'going with the flow,' if you'll excuse the expression."

"I guess I can overlook it this once," I replied. "But what if the conversation doesn't 'flow'?"

"That, I think, is Kismet. Fate. If you're not able to talk to each other easily, naturally, right from the start, then there's almost no chance anything too terrific is going to happen in the way of a romance later on. I know it may sound corny, but when people ask me what immediately attracts me to a woman, I have to say it's the way we're able to talk to each other. It's the way our speech patterns and rhythms sort of automatically fit together, as if we've known each other for a long time already. I can tell after talking to a woman for ten minutes if there's any chance whatsoever of our becoming friends or lovers. And I have never been wrong—a few times when I kept pushing it, thinking eventually things would click, that all we needed to do was to build up some common frame of reference, I wound up wasting a lot of time and effort. It simply didn't happen. Whenever I've met someone I *did* subsequently get involved with, for real, it was someone I'd been laughing with and comfortable with from the very first second we met."

"Love at first sight?"

"Love at first *sound*," Larry corrected me.

Among the many rights and privileges traditionally accorded to the male of the species, the right to initiate, to make the phone call that gets things started, has been perhaps the one most coveted by women. "If only I didn't have to sit around and wait for him to make the first move," women have often thought. "If only I could do the choosing instead of waiting to be chosen—and always by the wrong guy." The funny thing about all this, of course, is that men have long bemoaned the fact that they're the ones who have always had to read the signs and take the plunge, that they're the ones who have had to summon up their every ounce of courage and venture forth to a possible rebuff. If there's one masculine prerogative that they're only too willing to share these days, this is the one.

"As far as I'm concerned," says Gerald, "if women want to start making the calls, that's great. It looks like such a wonderful advantage, being the one to make the call instead of sitting around waiting to receive it, until you actually have to sit down and do it. That's when you see how hard it can be, to just hang your ego out there on the line, completely vulnerable and undefended. Frankly, I think being on the dialing end for a change will make women more sympathetic to the difficulties that men have had to deal with, and the problems that can crop up."

With acceptance, there's no problem; when a woman says yes to an invitation, it comes as a welcome relief, and a triumph. But when she says no, a man is usually left not only a little hurt, but somewhat confused to boot. Unless the reasons for the refusal have been carefully spelled out—and, I realize, those reasons are often as hard for the refuser to state as they are for the refusee to hear—he's left in the lurch, unsure whether he should press his suit and ask for another night, or simply drop the business altogether. He doesn't want to fail in his mission for want of but one more effort, nor does he want to further jeopardize his already wounded pride. He's left in the tricky position of trying to read the mind of someone who isn't even standing before him to see and study. All he's got is that disembodied voice coming out of the receiver at him, saying thanks so much for thinking of me, but I'm afraid I'm busy that night.

"The worst," says Gerald, "is when they're not interested in going out with you, but just to soften the blow, say maybe some other time. I know they're just trying to be kind, but it's impossible to know for sure, so you try them again a few days later, and then they only have to come up with some other excuse. If they really don't want to go out, then they ought to make that clear, one way or the other, the first time you call."

"That's all very well in theory," I said, "but would you really expect her to say, 'Sorry, but I find you totally unpalatable, don't bother me again.' Would you really want that kind of honesty?"

"Of course not," he replied, with some heat. "I would expect her to show some common decency, and *lie*. Tell me that she's already involved with someone. Even if I know it's untrue, I'm not going to grill her about it. I know that she's just tried to let me down easy, and I appreciate the gesture."

"Suppose she really does want to go out sometime, and it's just that she can't make it for the night you asked her?"

"In that case, I think she should suggest another time herself. She should say, 'I can't make it on Friday, but I really would like to get together sometime. How's next Wednesday for you?' Even if Wednesday's no good for me, at least now I know she's genuinely interested and that I'm not pursuing a lost cause."

But what about the woman making the call in the first place? Gerald claims he'd love it—as do most of the men I know. We all get calls from women who are our friends, suggesting a movie or a concert in the park, but even in this liberated day and age, very seldom do we get a call from someone new, someone who's expressly asking us out on what can only be defined as a date. No matter how many times they run that Harvey's Bristol Cream commercial where the woman in the satin pantsuit invites a man over for a drink, apparently the majority of women are still not entirely convinced that to do so is, in the words of the ad, "downright upright."

"As a rough estimate," says Larry, "I'd say it's happened to me never. The closest was when a woman I'd met only once called me up at the office, ostensibly about some business, and then just stayed on the phone with me until I sort of got the message and wound up asking her to lunch that afternoon."

"I take it your conversational styles merged together well?"

"As a matter of fact, smart guy, they did."

My own experiences with this bit of role reversal have been almost as numerous as Larry's. But I *can* think of one instance when a woman called me up for a date, and I can honestly say that during the short duration of that call I developed more sympathy and understanding for women than I had in the course of my entire previous lifetime. The woman who'd called had been going out with a good friend of mine for years, they'd recently broken up, and I had the distinct feeling she was calling me as a means of getting back at him. I politely declined her invitation, but coward that I am, I didn't put the total kibosh on the idea. So she, predictably, tried again the next week, I wriggled out of it again, and we both, of course, felt even worse. The third time she tried, I was finally prepared with an alibi, and explained that I was already seeing someone.

But what did I learn from this unfortunate episode? One, that it's flattering to be called; two, that it's depressing when it's not the right caller; and three, that it's very difficult indeed to be both honest and considerate. My hat is off to the women who have received unwelcome calls from me in the past without ever letting me know it. If women do begin dialing up men more often, I think we'll all benefit from the switch—at the same time that women begin to enjoy the pleasure of taking the initiative, they'll understand how daunting the prospect can sometimes be; at the same time that men bask in the glow that comes from being called, they'll also understand what diplomacy and care must sometimes be taken. Everyone, it seems to me, will gain by the exercise—and twice as many dates are likely to get made.

Who Gets the Check?

Wait a minute—I may have spoken too soon. When I said that calling up for a date was the one prerogative men were most willing to give up, I wasn't taking into account the privilege of *paying* for a date. That, too, I think, men are in most cases willing, if not anxious, to share. With the cost of a night out escalating at the same rate as the national defense budget, sharing the expenses has often become more than merely desirable—for a lot of men, it's become imperative. It's that, or sit home sorting socks every night.

Still, I'll concede that splitting the tab with a man can be almost as tricky as defusing a bomb. Most of us still carry at least a portion of our ego in our wallets, and if we can't blithely toss off a wad of bills, we feel everything from unsuccessful to undesirable. Much as our reason and "raised consciousness' may deny it, in some deeper part of our selves we still think of money, at least to a degree, as the measure of a man. If we have to ask a date to chip in, then we don't feel that we've quite measured up. And we can't help thinking that she thinks so, too.

On nights when sleep refuses to come, nights when I receive a parade of ghostly visitors to rival that of King Richard III on Bosworth Field (act 5, scene 3), I am invariably reminded of a date with a girl named Laurie, when I was 16 years old. I had wangled out of my parents the car keys, permission to stay out till one A.M., and 20 dollars to cover expenses. Piloting the car with all the care I had been taught in my driver's ed class, signaling each turn eight blocks ahead of time, cruising at a maximum speed of 25 miles per hour, we arrived in due course at the inexpensive dining spot I had selected after countless hours of deliberation. A printed sticker slathered across the glass door said "Closed until further notice," and was signed "The Board of Health."

"Gee," I said, all my plans suddenly crashing down around me, "it was always such a great place. Where would you like to go now?"

"Well, seeing as we've already parked the car and everything" (a parallel maneuver that I had executed with only minor damage to the front and back fenders), "why don't we just go across the street to that Mexican place, the Casa del

Sol? I've been there with my parents before, and it's pretty good."

Whether it was out of simple stupidity, or dread of having to move the car again, I agreed. We were seated by the maitre d', dressed in a black tuxedo, at the sort of table my obvious sophistication customarily commanded (directly facing the men's room) and presented with tasseled, velvet-covered menus roughly the size of movie screens. With my heart temporarily stopped dead in my chest, and a clammy sensation creeping over all my limbs, I cracked open the menu . . . peeked at the price list to the right . . . and suddenly felt myself inundated by a cool, refreshing tidal wave of relief.

"Hey," I said, rejoicing, "this place is very reasonable."

"Oh, good—I was just wondering if it wasn't going to be too much."

"No problem," I said, opening the menu a crack further, enough to notice now that the page I'd been looking at was labeled, in small letters in the upper left corner, "Appetizers." The page behind it—"Entrées"—carried the grim tidings.

The waiter appeared. "Would you like to order now?" he said, pencil poised for action.

"Are you ready?" Laurie asked, her eyes barely making it above the menu.

"You, uh, you go ahead," I replied. In mute horror, I listened as she ordered the house salad to start, a side dish of the Casa del Sol's special nachos—at the waiter's suggestion—a glass of white wine (wasn't he going to card her, for god's sake?), and the combination platter number one, known as El Conquistador—no doubt because you'd have to be Cortez to afford it. When she'd finished giving her order, and the waiter again trained his sights on me, I turned the menu toward him, and pointed at number 12. "I'll have that," I said quietly.

"The Peon Platter," he confirmed, his pencil scratching away. "What to start?"

"Nothing, thank you. I'm not really all that hungry."

"How about a salad? Nice, green salad, tomato, special house dressing?"

"All right, that'll be fine."

"To drink?"

"Water will be fine."

Having done all the damage he could, he snatched up the menus and departed.

"Are you feeling okay?" Laurie asked, leaning across the table.

"Fine, fine," I said, my brain clattering away like an adding machine. $5.90, plus $8.50, plus $2.00, twice, plus $3.00, plus $2.00 again—there was no way, no *way* I was going to make it. "Will you excuse me for a minute?"

Passing the maitre d' at the front door, I issued a chirpy "Be right back," then ran to a corner phone booth where I feverishly dialed the only friend I could think of who lived nearby. After ten or 12 rings, just as I was about to hang up, Ken answered.

"Thank God you're home," I said. "I've got big trouble. I'm at the Casa del Sol with—"

"Hoo-boy, big spender."

"With Laurie, and I'm not gonna be able to cover the check. Can you come over here right away and bring me as much money as you can get your hands on?" I could hear him thinking.

"As much money as I can get my hands on amounts to about $7.00. I'd be glad to *lend* it to you, but how am I supposed to get it to you?"

Now I could hear myself thinking. "Here's the story—I'll tell Laurie I called you since we were in the neighborhood, and asked you to stop by with a book I'd lent you that I need for a paper I'm writing. Stash the money under the front cover, and just hand me the book. No funny business, okay? We're sitting at the back of the main dining room, right across from the men's room. Hurry."

When I got back to the table, the salads and nachos were waiting. Laurie was sipping her wine. We'd made it about halfway through the main course when I saw Ken threading his way between the tables toward us. "Here's Ken with that book I told you about, the one that I needed."

"Hi ya, Laurie," he said, giving her an unnecessarily major kiss. "You look just great. Just great. What are you doing out with this goofball?"

Laurie laughed, I tried, Ken pulled a book from his back pocket. "Here's that book you wanted so badly," he said, placing squarely on the table a dog-eared paperback, with a solid yellow cover, entitled *Teenagers in Heat*. "Good luck with that 'paper' you're working on," he said. "'Night, Laurie. See you in French class."

The money, at least, was there. I slipped it out and put it in my pocket. I'd just make it now, I figured.

"You needed *that* book?" Laurie asked, clearly appalled.

"No, not really. It was actually something else I needed. This is just one of Ken's little jokes, I guess. I hope you didn't mind him kissing you like that. Ken can't get a date to save his life."

When we'd finished our main course, and the waiter, now my greatest nemesis, appeared again, I was ready for him.

"Dessert?" he said, extending the menus.

Leaning backwards in my chair, spreading my hands across my stomach, puffing out my cheeks and bulging my eyes, I groaned, "Not me. I'm stuffed. I couldn't eat another thing. How about you, Laurie? Do you think you can wedge in even one more tiny morsel of food? I *know* I can't."

"You enjoyed your dinner then?" said the waiter, beaming. "Was good?"

"Yes, wonderful," I said, "but so *much*."

"I know just what you need," he said, reassuringly. "Just right to finish with—two Casa del Sol special flan, very light, good for digestion. You will enjoy them," he said, winking broadly at Laurie. (What *was* this? I thought. A free-for-all?)

"Oh, yes, I love flan," said Laurie. "And could I have some coffee, too?"

"Two coffees," he jotted down merrily.

After the flan, after the coffee, after the waiter had suggested Laurie take with her the rose from the vase on the table, the check, appropriately entombed in a brown velvet folder, was discreetly placed at my elbow. Counting the spare change I'd found in my pocket, my total assets came to $27.94. With bated breath, I lifted the cover of the folder and glanced at the bottom of the check. $29.00 even. I felt like a gambler who'd just staked his all, and lost.

"What do you want to do now?" Laurie asked. "Do you want to go to a movie?"

"Yeah, maybe, I don't know," I muttered, distractedly. $29.00.

"Or would you rather just drive to the lake?" she suggested with a mischievous leer.

"Yeah, maybe."

"Well, you sure don't seem very enthusiastic."

"Laurie," I said, slowly raising my eyes to hers. "I have to tell you something."

"Yes?"

"I don't know how to say this. So I guess I'll just have to give it to you straight." She suddenly looked a little worried. "I can't pay this check."

"What do you mean?"

"I don't have enough money."

"Didn't your parents give you any credit cards?"

"No. And I need at least a few bucks."

"Boy, you had me scared there for a minute," she said, taking her purse off the back of her chair. "I guess I'm relieved that it's only this. All I've got," she said, opening her wallet, "is $5.00. Will that do it?"

"Barely."

Taking the money from her soft, pretty, innocent hand, I felt utterly disgraced. $29.00 even I slipped into the folder, the remaining $3.00 I left on the table as a tip. Coming around behind Laurie's chair, I pulled it out for her, and when she'd turned and walked a few steps away from the table, reached back, grabbed the tip (the car needed gas), and seeing the waiter advancing to clear the dishes, hurriedly escorted her out the door. We were already crawling away from the curb when Laurie remembered the book.

"Teenagers in Heat—you left it on the table. Do you want to go back?"

"No, that's all right," I said. Maybe the waiter will enjoy flipping through it over a plate of the Casa del Sol's special nachos, I thought.

In retrospect, the whole episode seems not much more than silly. But at the time, it was devastating. I made light of it all evening long, but as soon as I got back to my bedroom that night I buried my face in the pillow, overwhelmed with humiliation. My little brother, who shared the room, taunted me with "What's wrong—wouldn't Laurie kiss you goodnight?" and even pummeling him soundly did nothing to assuage my pain (though it certainly added to his).

By the time I'd gone through a couple of semesters of college, I'd begun to feel a little more comfortable with the notion of a woman sharing the expenses. Somehow in college, everything seemed so egalitarian—we were all in the same boat there, wearing the same jeans and workshirts, living in the same dorms, sleeping through the same lectures. It was universally understood that no one ever had any money, and that if we planned to have any fun at all, we'd have to pool our resources. And nothing was very expensive anyway—we ate cheese pizza, drank generic beer, and watched movie classics sponsored by the campus film society.

That "we're all in this together" attitude lingered on, at least for a while, after I'd moved to New York. Most of the women I met and went out with were also in their early 20s, and we all worked at entry-level jobs that didn't pay terribly well. Our apartments were virtually interchangeable, all furnished with the battered bureaus, curling posters, and India-print bedspreads that had once adorned our college rooms. A night out still consisted of homemade chili, eaten off paper plates, and then maybe a stop-off at a cheap, outdoor cafe where we could carefully nurse one drink apiece for an hour or so. To this day, I find myself leaving one swallow in my glass, or one bite on my dessert plate, until the very second that I'm ready to leave a restaurant.

But over the past few years, things have almost imperceptibly begun to revert somewhat, it seems to me. Once again, I find myself going unchallenged for the check; once again, I notice that in matters of finance, I am generally in charge. Whether this is due to the waning of women's liberation fervor, the soaring cost of a veal cutlet, or the simple assumption, on the part of my female companions, that as a "best-selling author" (so, sometimes I lie) I can afford it, I can't say for sure. What I do know is that my wallet is getting a much more thorough work-out these days.

I also find that I'm being forced, against my basic nature, into telling the truth. If I represent myself as that "best-selling author" too often, my dates come to expect some pretty extravagant entertainments; if I don't deliver, I look like a cheapskate, or a fraud. If, on the other hand, I go the route of the "poor, struggling artiste," I save money, certainly, but I lose not only some dates, but a good deal of cachet, too. After a certain age, I've discovered, being a poor, struggling artiste—or a poor, struggling anything, for that matter—is no longer hip, or winning. In the eyes of the world, not to mention your parents, it's time to have arrived.

"Yes, I guess I am paying almost all the time now," said a banker friend named Phil, to whom I often unburden myself on money matters. "I guess I never noticed till you brought it up. But now that I'm a vice-president at the bank" (Phil never fails to work this into a conversation), "it's not any kind of problem. And it's definitely an improvement over squabbling over the check. I always hated that 'going Dutch' business. 'Who had the melba toast, who had the extra drink?' It's so petty, and undignified. Checks should never be split; if a woman really wants to keep things equal, she should simply ask me out for another time, or buy us a couple of concert tickets, or something."

Even as a non-v.p., I agree wholeheartedly. There's nothing like running your finger down a column of figures to kill the romance in an evening. The person who suggested the dinner ought to be the one who pays for it. The other should find some more interesting way, if he or she so chooses, to repay the host. Personally, as someone who would rather juggle hand grenades than scramble an egg, I much appreciate an invitation to a home-cooked meal, complete with candlelight, soft music, and no captains, wine stewards, or waiters to contend with.

When a woman *does* want to treat a man to dinner, she can make the occasion infinitely more comfortable for him by paying the check with a credit card rather than cash. I know it may sound like a trivial distinction, but there's just something about a woman whipping out her purse and tossing cold, hard cash onto the table that makes a man feel . . . conspicuous. A card, unobtrusively presented, and whisked away by the waiter, is far less traumatic; using plastic, as we are all reminded later when we receive our monthly statement and collapse on the floor in shock, is almost like no money is involved at all. Your guest will find it much easier to take, and so will you—like a dinosaur that has stubbed its toe, you won't really get the message until long after the accident is over, and by then, the pain may be somewhat dulled.

Once a relationship is actually underway, most, if not all, of these questions become superfluous. Every couple settles into its own particular financial arrangement, depending upon such factors as respective incomes, general operating expenses, relative stinginess, etc. Once the "dating phase" is over, everything relaxes, and some sort of unspoken agreement is usually reached—I pay for dinners, you pay for the cabs. Whatever.

"The best thing about 'settling in,'" says a woman named Rachel, who happens to live right across the hall from me, "is that you don't have to worry anymore about what you owe a guy, or what *he* thinks you owe him, for buying you dinner. Much more often than I care to remember, I had the distinct feeling that the more a guy spent on me in the course of an evening, the more he expected me to pay him back later, in a different coin, shall we say. That's probably the major reason I started paying my own way a lot of the time—just so I wouldn't be beholden to him, or feel obligated in any way.

"In fact," she added, "if men were smarter, I think they'd realize that when a woman absolutely *insists* on paying her share, especially on a first or second date, it's usually a pretty clear message that she's not interested in getting involved with him. Personally, I hate to incur any debts whatsoever that I'm not prepared to pay off."

Phil the banker, when I subsequently recounted this to him, nodded his head sagely, and said, "Very solid advice, and well put. Sounds like she has a good head on her shoulders, this neighbor of yours. By the way, what else can you tell me about her?"

Strange and wonderful, isn't it, what will kindle romantic interest?

The Unwelcome Advance

Indirectly, however, my neighbor Rachel has touched on another fairly sensitive topic. What *do* you do, at the end of a date, with a guy who seems to feel that you owe him something? How do you handle, deftly and diplomatically, an unwelcome advance?

"You already know how I handle it," said Rachel, with a laugh. About a week earlier, I'd come home late one night and found her standing in front of her door, in the company of a huge palooka. His arms were planted against either side of the door jamb, with Rachel right between them. At first, thinking I was intruding on a tender romantic tableau, I scooted past as fast as I could, digging my keys out of my pocket. But when Rachel blurted out, "Hi, Robert, where were you tonight?" from beneath the great arch of his arms, I sensed I might have been wrong.

"The ice cream parlor," I said, holding up my pistachio cone as proof.

"Robert, I'd like you to meet . . . what is it you prefer to be called? Gabe? Gabriel?"

"Gabriel," he replied, dryly, and only slowly dropping his arms from the door. Since I'd already decided I didn't like him, I extended my hand, sticky with ice cream.

"Pleased to meet you," I said.

"Gabriel and I went to the Fassbinder retrospective. What do you think of his films?"

Though my knowledge of Fassbinder could have easily fit into my ice cream cone, I managed to hold forth for a minute or two, while Gabriel's face clouded over with increasing frustration and boredom. His discomfort gave me renewed strength, and I soon discovered that I knew all sorts of fascinating things about German cinema that I'd never known I knew before. Rachel's expression signaled to me her immense relief, and everytime it looked like my comments were running out, she quickly popped in with another question. We were deeply engrossed in an utterly meaningless conversation when Gabriel's patience finally broke.

"Excuse me," he said, turning to Rachel. "I thought maybe we could have a drink together. *Inside.*"

"Oh, gosh," she said, "I'm afraid I don't have a single thing to drink in the house. I'm so sorry. Maybe some other time." And whipping around, she plunged her key into the lock, swung open the door, and closed it again with a cheery "Goodnight all!" at something approaching the speed of light. As we listened to the sound of her deadbolt being driven home, Gabriel slowly turned the full weight of his menace on me.

"I'm afraid I'm all out, too," I mumbled, scurrying into my own apartment.

While Rachel had indeed displayed an exemplary presence of mind, she had also been very lucky that time around. She just happened to have a friendly male neighbor, who'd shown up at precisely the right moment. Such good fortune can only be accepted, when it comes, with ineffable gratitude; it can never be counted on. (After all, I don't go out for ice cream more than twice a week.) So, in the absence of luck or coincidence, it's a good idea to have some alternative plans for dealing with the occasional masher.

The most important thing is to know your own mind. Check in with yourself regularly during the course of the date to see how you're feeling about the guy, and the prospects for later in the evening. Are you really enjoying yourself? Would you want to go out with him again sometime? Are you "in the mood" for love? If so, by all means proceed. If not, then start taking the necessary steps to establish some distance between you. I'm not suggesting that you transform yourself into a veritable block of ice; just look to see that you're not sending out any erroneously affectionate signals.

Much of the time, men may misinterpret (I suppose because they want to) a touch on the arm, or a look that lingers. They're always scouting for signs that you're interested in them, and depending on their own eagerness, they may mistake the most innocuous comment, or casual gesture, as a token of your interest. Even if you simply catch your heel on a sidewalk grate and stumble against him, he may suspect you planned the whole thing and duly chalk it up on his own internal toteboard. Of course, accidents and misinterpretations you can't anticipate or plan for; if he jumps to an illogical or unfounded conclusion, that's his problem. But by deliberately monitoring your own conduct as best you can, you'll find that if the evening does wind up in an unwelcome wrestling match, at least you won't have yourself to blame for it in any way whatsoever. And certain knowledge of your own innocence will treble your strength and bravery, should a showdown occur.

Of course, the best strategies are those that allow no opportunity for the showdown to arise in the first place. "If I'm not interested in him," says my friend Lisa, "as soon as we leave the theater or restaurant or party, I thank him for the evening, plead utter exhaustion, and stick out my arm to flag down the first cab I see. Most men, however, won't either (a) take the hint, or (b) allow me to go home unescorted. So then, as soon as we get in the cab, I say to the driver, very distinctly, 'Your first stop will be at Seventieth and Second Avenue (where I live), and you'll be going on from there.'"

"What if you've been out in the guy's own car all night?"

"Not much difference, really, except that I've learned to check the door handle when I get in. Sometimes it seems to me that every car today has got its very own kind of lever or crank, and I've had two or three otherwise graceful exits spoiled for me when I had to fumble and push at an unfamiliar handle."

If you're expecting your date to make an advance that you'd really rather he didn't, do anything you can to keep him from escorting you all the way to your apartment (or house) door. Try to leave him at the curbside, or in the building lobby. If you do wind up at the door together (as is often unavoidable), get out your key, but before using it, turn to face him, and mustering all your courage, say something like you'd invite him in, but the place is a mess, or you don't want to wake your roommate (if you're really smart, you'll have invented a roommate earlier in the evening), or whatever else springs to mind. Say goodnight, briskly turn to the door, and don't look back as you slip inside. If you then wish to breathe an audible sigh of relief, you're entitled, but in deference to the guy who may still be standing flat-footed in the hallway just outside, try to keep the volume down.

Unfortunately, most men (particularly those accustomed to pressing their case) are prepared for this doorway ploy, and if they see no other way of being invited in, they'll politely ask if they can use your bathroom for a minute before taking off. It's a hard request to refuse: what do you say, that you have no indoor plumbing?

Once inside the apartment, the potential masher figures he's home free. When he emerges from the bathroom, he'll wander into the living room and start a diversionary conversation about anything at all, the painting over your piano—"Did you paint that? I really like it"—the rug on the floor—"Great rug, my mother used to have a lot of great rugs at her place"—or the afghan draped across the back of the sofa—"Did you make that? I really like it." Fascinating as these conversational gambits may be, do not be drawn in; the next thing you know, you'll be squirming your way out of an amorous half-nelson on the sofa. Instead, stand, sentinel-like, by the half-open front door, perhaps thumbing through the day's mail, or flipping through your pocket appointment book, until he comes out of the bathroom and discovers that you meant business—and not hanky-panky—all along.

There are going to be times, however, when your best-laid plans go awry, or when the most mild-mannered fellow, invited over for a home-cooked meal, suddenly becomes an octopus of passion, attempting to entwine you in his persistent limbs. There are times when a man just won't take "no" for an answer, times when he'll offer up, in the feverish heat of his attack, some of the most heart-rending and ridiculous appeals you could imagine. There is, for instance, the old "I just can't control myself—your beauty is so irresistible" approach. Just remind yourself—and him—that if he could control himself when you had lunch at his office cafeteria last Thursday, he can do the same now.

Or the "I can't stop myself now—a man can hurt himself, physically, if he stops after a certain point" argument. Though not generally heard from anyone significantly past puberty, there is both good news and bad news on this score. The bad news is that there is no known cure for the condition (commonly known as "blue balls"); the good news is that there is no such condition.

Or the "Sorry, I certainly didn't mean to shock you—I thought we were both adults here" tactic, designed to make you feel like a backward child for not falling in line with his wishes. Of all the various approaches, this is probably the easiest of all to deal with, because it is also the most likely to provoke you to fury. While it's easy for a man to make a pass when it isn't really wanted, while it's common for a man to push his luck a little further than he sometimes ought to, only an idiot, or a bully, relentlessly charges forward, again and again, in the face of clear and increasing opposition. If you've stopped being overly polite about the whole business, if you've stopped trying to spare his feelings, if you've decided, without any doubts, that you don't want what he wants, then speak your mind—"I don't want to make love with you"—and get up. Move to another chair if you think he can cool down and be civil again. If you think he's already too far gone for that, then starchy as it may seem, you may as well show him to the door. Don't feel guilty—you haven't done anything wrong. And absolutely, don't feel silly—refusing to be manhandled, or inveigled into sex, isn't childish or prudish or unkind. Once he's actually gone, you may feel a little odd, thinking "What just went on here?" But think how you'd feel next morning, if you'd let him browbeat you into doing something that you hadn't wanted to do? Losing your respect for him is bad enough; losing respect for yourself is a lot more serious.

Blind Date Roulette

Into every social life, no matter how full, there must inevitably come, once in awhile, a barren stretch, a time when you've just broken up with one person and haven't as yet found a suitable replacement. A time when, no matter how hard you look, you can't seem to spot any new and appealing face on the horizon, no enticing new someone in the next office at work, no alluring neighbor who's just moved in across the hall. A time when even your old address book, carefully combed over, yields no potentially revivable name, no old flame that could be brought back to life with a little effort. And into every social life, at just such times, there's bound to come, sooner or later, a call from that friend to whom you have earlier unburdened your heart.

"How are you doing?" she asks, gently and solicitously, as if speaking to an invalid.

"Fine," you say. "I finally got that raise I was waiting for."

"Hey, that's great," your friend replies, as if by reflex. "But that's not what I meant. I meant socially—have you two gotten back together again, by any chance?"

"No," you say, instantly plummeting back into your depressed state.

"That's all I wanted to know—now listen, I don't think it's a great idea for you to just keep moping around the house every night. I think you should be going out, having some fun, forgetting about what happened."

"Sure—but who with?"

With those very words, you have sprung the trap, you have articulated exactly what your friend was waiting to hear all along.

"Well, it's funny you should say that—because I happen to know this super guy, who's just moved to the city, and I think you two would really hit it off. Now, listen, I hope you don't mind, but I've already told him a little bit about you, and he said why not, he'd be glad to get together anytime next week that you're free. So what do you say, how about it?"

The question is this: How do *you* react to such an offer? Do you remain a calm, mature, rational adult, asking your friend only pertinent, intelligent questions about your prospective blind date? Or do you (like me) immediately think of catching the next flight to Bolivia? Do you sensibly inquire about the arrangements for the date, and agree to do it, or do you instantly start making excuses, saying you've discovered the joy and true peace of mind that come from unalloyed celibacy, that you've decided to buy a dog instead, that before you go out with anyone new, you're waiting for a huge zit on your chin to disappear? Do you respond with curiosity and courage . . . or timidity and tremors?

If with courage, congratulations; you rank in the 99th percentile. If with terror, welcome to the rest of us. Blind dates, innocuous as they may seem in the abstract, in the concrete have the ability to make most of us jumpy, jittery, and just plain bananas. The very suggestion stirs up a potent batch of conflicting emotions. Since the times when our friends are most likely to try fixing us up are also the times when our own self-esteem is most likely to be at low ebb, we don't exactly relish the idea of being sized up on the doorstep by some total stranger. All our worst insecurities are currently bubbling to the surface . . . and taking shape, as it were, in that life-threatening zit. This, we feel, is no time to be taking any chances.

Nor is it any time to start being treated like a charity case by our friends. Irrational though it may be, it's easy to feel a trifle insulted when a friend suggests fixing you up. "Do they really think I couldn't find a date if I wanted one?" you say to yourself with some indignation. "Do they really think they have to dig somebody up for me?" In your heart, you know that they're only trying to be helpful, but sometimes you have to kick yourself, hard, to remember that.

Why? Because blind dates, let's face it, do not have the best reputation around. A blind date is generally considered a joke, a last resort, a running gag with familiar lines like "She's got a great personality," or "He's not as bald as he looks." Blind dates have a serious public relations problem because the people doing the fixing-up do not, by and large, take their job seriously enough, and because the people *being* fixed-up take the whole business *too* seriously.

Take the case of my friend Patricia, for instance, who recently broke up with her boyfriend of four years standing. One of her office-mates, someone who was also presumably her friend, offered to fix her up, and Patricia, though normally a wary sort, agreed. She figured her colleague knew her pretty well—knew she was artsy, knew, above all, that she was extraordinarily sensitive about her height (a shade under six feet)—and just naturally assumed that the guy her friend had in mind for her would at least fit the bill on those basics.

"Wrong, on both counts," as she explained it to me afterwards. "The guy was a certified public accountant—which he told me no less than 14 times—and he had all of Dudley Moore's dimensions, with none of his personality or charm. For the first hour or so, I kept bending over to hear what he was saying, feeling more and more like a giraffe all the time, but once I actually heard him announce, as if he'd just thought of it, that he didn't know much about art, but he knew what he liked, I stopped bothering. You know, it's at times like that that I'm thankful for every inch I've got."

If we assume that Patricia's office-mate started out with no evil intentions, then we are left with only one other conclusion—that, like most matchmakers, she had made the fatal mistake of approaching her task, one that requires the utmost tact and consideration, with about the same degree of attention normally devoted to watching a detergent commercial. She had unhesitatingly slapped together two people—two fragile and vulnerable egos—with no more thought than you'd use to toss cold cuts and cheese into an open hoagie roll. She was clearly under the impression common among matchmakers (particularly those that are married themselves) that any date at all is better than none, that any company whatsoever is preferable to solitude. It's an erroneous assumption, as far as I'm concerned (I can have a very good time by myself), but there's just no convincing some people of that.

Just as there's no convincing others, that once they've agreed to *go* on a blind date, they shouldn't be demanding, or expecting, to meet the most wonderful, perfectly suited individual in the world. If they go into it thinking the date is a bust if they don't wind up engaged, then the date is going to be a bust. Blind dates must be approached in the spirit of adventure, as an opportunity to meet someone who would not otherwise have been met, someone you might never have chosen to go out with on your own. It's a chance to try your wings in a new context, in a way you don't usually see yourself. And no matter what happens, no matter how insufficient the chemistry is between you, it is, after all, only for the one evening, and really, how bad can it be? I mean, even Patricia, now that it's over, seems to thoroughly enjoy telling the story of her disastrous date with the miniature accountant. And who knows—for that matter, he may be dining out on it, too.

The Poacher's Tale

After ten years, it's a miracle to me that Bert is still my friend. But more than a miracle really, I think it's a living testament to the uncommon skill, tact, and civility that I've displayed while absconding with one girlfriend of his after another. Not that I'm proud of what I've done—I'll be the first to admit that swiping a friend's sweetheart, poaching on a friend's preserves, as it were, is a pretty tacky bit of behavior. But still, I must be managing it with a certain degree of grace, since Bert and I had a perfectly amicable dinner together just last Thursday night, after which I went over to see Robin, who, needless to say, was going out with Bert when I first met her.

For me, Bert has proved to be an absolute godsend. Unlike most folks, who spend their days in busy, well-populated offices, I work alone, in my apartment. The only person I ever meet there is the exterminator, on the second Tuesday of every month. My neighbors are illegal aliens, who speak languages I can't even begin to identify, and little old ladies who've held their present leases since the Spanish–American War. I don't enjoy singles bars, and I refuse to enroll in a modern dance class. So I ask you, what does this leave me? How else should I go about meeting women, if not through the agency of my close friends?

Now I realize that all this may sound like I'm just trying to justify my reprehensible conduct. And that's right, I am. But if we were all to display this same kind of exemplary honesty, who among us could claim _never_ to have been attracted to a friend's mate, _never_ to have seriously considered—or even gone ahead with—getting that coveted third party all for our very own? Of all the ways to meet people with whom we're likely to hit it off, what can beat an introduction from a mutual friend? And what higher recommendation can that trusted friend offer than to be romantically involved with the person himself?

Of course, we've all got friends who persistently go out with people we detest. But to Bert's great misfortune (and my own good fortune) he and I have remarkably similar tastes: warm, witty, willowy women. To make matters worse (for

Bert) and better (for me) he and I are also quite alike—thin, bearded, intellectual (provided you don't listen too closely). Women who go for Bert find that I am but one small step away. That's where the differences between us come into play.

Bert is a doctor with an overpowering social conscience; I'm a writer oblivious to any suffering that is not my own—in which case I believe it to be of national importance. Bert is an aspiring gourmet cook; I have only recently learned to distinguish between a spatula and a flyswatter. Bert believes in jogging and keeping in shape; I have run only twice in my life, and both times I was being chased. (For those of you who wish to contact Bert at this point, I'll be glad to forward any mail.) But suffice it to say, the heart works in mysterious ways, and on three separate occasions women in apparently full possession of their senses have chosen to give up Bert's pectorals and homemade paté for the dubious pleasures of sloth and Stouffer's. I will cite, as evidence, just the most recent example—Robin.

Robin and I met at one of Bert's Saturday-night bashes, in his cavernous apartment on the Lower East Side. Though I'd like to remember our first encounter in a more romantic light, we, in fact, met while standing in line for the bathroom. The line was long, it moved slowly, and by the time my turn arrived, I was already so taken with her that, against all precedent, I allowed her to go ahead of me. A greater sacrifice I could not have made.

When I'd emerged myself, I happened to bump into an old friend, Jack, to whom I instantly confided the good news. "I just met this terrific girl," I said. "That one right over there," I said, pointing out Robin, who was now dancing up a storm in the next room.

"The one in the plaid shirt?" he said.

"Yes."

"And the jeans?"

"Uh-huh."

"You mean Robin?"

"That's right—I *thought* that's what she said her name was. You know her then?"

"A little. But Bert knows her real well," he said, laying one consolatory hand upon my shoulder. "She's his girlfriend."

Bert had indeed been going out with her for a month or so, I later learned. But since she and I worked in the same general business—Robin was a copywriter at a publishing house—we did arrange to have a perfectly harmless *business* lunch the next week. Followed by a perfectly harmless movie a few days later (business again, since her company had published the film's novelization). We had business drinks a couple of times, and one Friday night we attended a business party together (after all, *someone* there might have been an editor somewhere). And so it went, business, business, business, until Robin finally broke it off with Bert and we suddenly discovered, in one of those moments of rare clarity, that we were now going out with each other.

But how, you may ask, was I able to sleep at night? Can the head of a poacher ever rest easy on the pillow? Well, to that I'd say, it all depends. It's very important for a poacher to keep in mind certain old axioms, like "All's fair in love and war," "To the victor go the spoils," and "Nice guys finish last." These can all help to soothe the troubled spirit and assuage the guilty conscience—as can the sure and certain knowledge that nobody was ever successfully stolen away (even Robin) who wasn't already predisposed to be. Yes, the poacher may indeed have carried off a prize, but chances are the prize had been ready and waiting to be carried off for quite some time.

For the novice, however, who's contemplating trying a little poaching of his or her own, there *are* a couple of questions that ought to be seriously considered first. For one, there are your own motivations to think about—are you about to perform this maneuver simply out of boredom, or sexual desperation? Are you poaching from a friend just because you're too lazy to go out and look for someone new on your own? Are you doing it just for the challenge? Or worse, because in some subconscious way you're angry with your friend? Plumb your motives, and if any of these turn up, think again before going ahead with your plan.

There's only one good, or at least defensible, reason for poaching, and that's a genuine and hard-to-resist attraction to the person you're thinking of stealing. Ideally, you should have detected a reciprocal gleam in the eye of that same special someone. If you *do* feel that the spark is there, then, and only then, should you consider fanning it into a flame.

"The spark was definitely there," says my friend Sally, "before I'd even thought about 'poaching,' as you call it. But my situation was probably a whole lot more complicated than most, because at the time I met David, he was going out with Jenny, and Jenny was my roommate! We shared a tiny, two-room apartment, and a lot of times when David called, Jenny would be out. David and I would just start talking, and before we knew it half an hour would have gone by. Then, once or twice, he stopped by the apartment before Jenny got home from work, and we'd have some coffee together. The chemistry between us was always very good, and to tell you the truth, I thought it was better than what he had with Jenny right from the start. I knew I wanted to go out with him, but I didn't know what, if anything, I could do about it, until I got invited to this formal party through work. David was the only guy I knew who owned a tuxedo, Jenny was away visiting her family that week, and to make a long story short, I called him and asked if he'd like to go with me. About three weeks later, we 'went public' with the fact that we were now seeing each other."

"How'd Jenny react to the news?"

"Not real well, I'm afraid. Not that I blame her. I moved to a new place, of course, and only now, about nine months later, are she and I *starting* to be friends again. She's got a new boyfriend, which has helped a lot, and I try to say as little as possible about Dave."

Unfortunately, there's just no way to poach without threatening the friendship—and that's precisely why it's never worth trying if all that you're after is a brief bit of fun, or a one-night stand. Nor can you hope to keep it a secret for long. Time and the grapevine will always do their work. In my own case, for instance, word had soon filtered back to Bert, no doubt through my old friend Jack, that Robin and I were "keeping company." Which in Bert's view, thank God, was just fine—as far as he was concerned, I was just an awfully decent guy, who'd picked up one of his cast-offs and was doing what he could to help her through that necessary period of mourning for the relationship. It made no difference that Robin had been the one to call it quits with him; he'd already rewritten that portion of the script. The way he remembered it now, *he* was the one who'd ended the affair.

It is this curious tendency to tamper with history, to render it more congenial to the needs of the ego, that the veteran poacher learns to rely on. The victim may be counted on to reconstruct past events in such a way that he no longer appears, to himself or the world, ever to have been victimized at all. Which is, of course, precisely the way the poacher would like things to appear, too. In the end, everybody's happy, and Bert and I, for example, can continue to have dinner, go to a ballgame, go out drinking—do all the things we've always done together. If there's been any change at all, and I'm undoubtedly just imagining this, it's that Bert now seems scrupulously to avoid mentioning anything at all about anyone he's going out with.

But then, come to think of it, so do I.

___Why Didn't He Call Back?___

But poaching is nothing, a mere misdemeanor at best, compared to the major felony I'm about to bring up. If there's any one bit of male behavior that drives most of the women I know truly crazy, one particular riddle that they wrestle with in vain, one sore point to which their thoughts endlessly return, like a tongue to a jagged tooth, to probe and investigate, it's got to be this: Why do men—men who appear to be genuinely interested, attentive, perhaps even smitten—men whom you have only just met, or men you have already gone out with once, twice, maybe a few times—promise, with seeming sincerity, to call again, and then, like a card from a conjurer's hand, vanish—pouf!—into thin air? Why do they say it, if they don't mean it, and why, if they do mean it, don't they do it? What, in short, gives?

"Once upon a time," says my friend Patricia, "I was actually so young and naive and foolish as to sit around and wait by the phone after a guy had said he'd call me. I used to think that if I left my apartment for ten minutes to pick up my clothes at the dry cleaner that that's when my phone was ringing, that that's when he was trying to reach me. I can actually remember a couple of times when I turned down invitations from women friends of mine to do something over the weekend, because I was sure some guy was going to call any minute and that I'd be busy. In fact, you want to hear something really amazing? You know that blind date I had, the one with the munchkin accountant? Even *he* said he'd call me again."

"He didn't, did he?" I asked.

"No, of course not. I don't think he'd had any more fun that night than I did. I'm only saying that there it was, 'I'll call you,' popping up like some weird kind of reflex."

"You know something," I said. "I think that's exactly what it was. And much as I hate to admit it, I've done it myself."

Patricia looked at me with great disappointment. "You, too?"

"Me, too," I replied.

I can understand that accountant, standing under the canopy at Pat's apartment building, fidgeting, wondering what to say next, aware no doubt that the evening had not been a great success, but unsure about how, gracefully, to bring it to a close. I can understand how, in a misguided attempt to sign off pleasantly, he might have jumped up for a quick peck on the cheek, and then blurted out something like "Thanks—I'll call you," before hailing a passing cab. It's often uttered that thoughtlessly, that heedlessly, that "reflexively," as Pat would say. And it's certainly not intended to mislead or harm anyone. Translated, it might almost mean no more than "Thanks for the evening," or "Nice to have met you." It can spring to a man's lips with the same ease and alacrity.

And in today's superheated social atmosphere, where we all rocket around, bonding and splitting like so many loose particles in an atomic reactor, it frequently has occasion to. What *should* he say, a man often wonders, at the end of a date that hasn't gone as well as he'd hoped? Even if he knows that you're no more anxious than he is to repeat the experience, still he feels that there's no need to acknowledge that unfortunate truth, to drag it out in the open where it will only cause even more embarrassment to everyone concerned. So, in the hope of wrapping everything up in a muzzy ball of niceties and optimism, he burbles "I'll call you next week," not thinking for a minute that his words or sentiment will be taken literally.

"Sometimes I don't know how *not* to say it," comments my friend Ralph. "Even if I've just met somebody at one of those 'happy hour' bars near the firm, I don't know how else to end an encounter sometimes. To just pick up my briefcase and leave seems so rude, it's like admitting that our conversation hasn't been that interesting to me, or that she hasn't been. So I wind up exchanging phone numbers with her, or where we work, and I say I'll call, even though I know that I won't, and for the next few weeks I go to a different bar after work."

"Haven't you ever said you'll call, and meant it, and still not called in the end?"

"Oh, yes, plenty of times. Sometimes it's just because I lack the guts—I'm not sure she'll remember me, or that she liked me when we met. Sometimes it's procrastination—you know, you let it go for awhile because you're busy with work, and before you know it, weeks, or even months, have gone by, and it just doesn't seem like such a good idea anymore. And sometimes, if it's someone I've gone out with a few times, but I've realized that things aren't going anywhere, I have a tendency to sort of 'drop away.' I know that I should arrange for a face-to-face confrontation, or at least call and explain, but I can't bear the thought of actually doing it. Of actually conducting this grim post-mortem of the affair. I always think that she must be as aware of the failure as I am, and that calling back is only going to make us verbalize it all, and possibly inflict even more unnecessary damage on each other. And what's the good of that?"

None, of course—if damage *were* all that came of it. That the woman deserves to be apprised of what's going on, sometimes doesn't occur to men; and that she would *prefer* to know occurs to them almost never. Women are still, for many men, frail, fragile, and vulnerable creatures, not entirely fit for the thousand natural shocks that flesh is heir to, to be spared, if possible, any hurtful news. Believing that—or at least professing to believe it—also turns out to be very convenient: While telling themselves that they're only sparing the feelings of the helpless females, the men can in fact manage to spare their own feelings, and shield themselves from any chance of an argument, or a reproach. It's a neat trick, and a nice rationalization, when you get right down to it, for what is basically not much more than a good old-fashioned case of cowardice. But it does work.

Ironically, the swift and streamlined way in which affairs of the heart move along today is also responsible, I think, for a lot of the early derailments. Sexually, that first encounter is more likely than any other to go awry somehow—yes, it's exciting to go to bed with someone new for the first time, but it's also often problematical. Neither one of you knows what the other likes, or dislikes, neither one of you (unless terribly uninhibited or drunk) feels completely free to let loose and fully indulge him or herself. If the earth fails to move that first or second time you go to bed together, it's easy for a man to start thinking that some essential element must be missing from the relationship, or to start worrying that he's not quite measuring up, in your eyes or his own, between the sheets. Whatever the exact message coursing through his addled pate, the result is still the same: He decides not to call back.

Other men, notoriously, disappear because you've failed, as they would no doubt express it, "to put out." "It's what you'd call a classic 'no-win' situation," says my friend Bonnie, who works downtown in one of the Soho art galleries. "I've tried both approaches, and both of them got me nowhere. So much for strategy. With one man, an artist who's displayed at our gallery for years, I had a really nice—I thought—working relationship. We always had interesting talks, on the phone and in person, and one day, just as we'd finished hanging some new paintings he'd done, he asked me if I'd like to go to an opening with him. For about one second, I wondered whether I ought to socialize with a client, but then I thought, why not? What else have I got to do? So we went to the opening, and then to the Spring Street bar with some friends of his, and then he asked me back to his studio to see some new paintings he was doing. I know what it sounds like—and that's exactly what it was. He's a pretty good-looking guy, and a fairly successful artist, and I guess he's just used to sleeping with whomever he goes out with. But that's not really how I was thinking of him—I mean, I still thought of us as sort of professional acquaintances. I didn't object to the *idea* of sleeping with him—I just thought that since we saw each other all the time, at the gallery and everything, that it could wait a bit. I didn't want him to think that I was just another one of those artist groupies who crawl all over anybody who smells of turpentine. So anyway, I 'resisted his advances'—my mother would love to hear me say that—and from that point on he was not only cool and brusque on the phone to me whenever he called the gallery, but when he stopped by he'd make a point of dealing only with my boss, or the other assistant. He did *not*—surprise, surprise—ask me out again.

"Anyway, the upshot is even funnier—bad choice of words, I should probably say even more tragic. I really started to wonder, after that debacle, if I wasn't sufficiently 'with it,' if maybe I wasn't acting a little too high-minded about this whole sex business. So when one of our European dealers, a real smoothie, called me for a date a few weeks later, I was fully prepared to *get* with it. He took me to an arts benefit, and then we went back to his suite at the Plaza—room service champagne, cold lobster canapes—followed by you know what. And this time, I was fully cooperative, completely with it. And guess what? By the very next morning, I could *tell* he'd written me off as just another easy American lay. He didn't really want to have to talk to me over his coffee and croissant, and he had this insulting air of the conqueror about him. If he *had* called me again, I would never have agreed to go out with him, but the point of the story is, he never did."

On the surface of it, we do have what appears to be a clear case of "damned if you do, damned if you don't"; some guys, like the artist, can't take no for an answer, and some, like the dealer, can't take yes. If you do go to bed right off the bat, you risk being thought of, even in this thoroughly enlightened day and age, as cheap, or easy, or just not worthy of serious consideration; and if you don't, you can wind up labeled anything from an unsophisticated hayseed to a manipulative tease. And whichever verdict is ultimately handed down, one thing remains true—the follow-up call, again, doesn't come.

But may I venture to say that in both of the instances above, you're better off if it doesn't? Maybe men like the ones Bonnie has encountered lately aren't a small minority—much as I'd like to think so—but they are, without a doubt, not worth any trouble on your part. If his interest abates as soon as he discovers you're not ready to hop in the sack with him, he's never going to be exactly a pillar of support and affection, is he? And if, on the other hand, he treats you with subtle, or overt, contempt for having foolishly succumbed to his blandishments, then the next thing you know he'll be suggesting that you ply your charms for pecuniary goals, so to speak. If you ask me, I'd take my phone off the hook after going out with either one of these types.

One thing, I suppose, should be said for them, however— at least their motives are fairly easy to understand. When they don't call, at least you know why. A lot of other men disappear, even after things have begun to go quite well between you, for somewhat more mysterious reasons. In fact, the most common reason of all is probably just that—that things *have* begun to go well. There's nothing like a possibly successful relationship getting underway to send some men flying for cover.

Why? Because for many men words like Involvement and Commitment ring in their heads like death knells, and rather than allow things to get out of hand, they shut down any relationship at all as soon as it shows any signs whatsoever of flourishing. "Nip it in the bud, *now,*" flashes across their brain-pan, "before you find yourself with a wife, a mortgage, and one of those Ford stationwagons with woodgrain on the side. Get going!" Unfortunately, in the extremity of their terror, such men often neglect to take a few moments out from packing their bags and making their flight reservations, to call you up and explain just *why* they're planning to evaporate from your life. Though even if they did make the call, they'd have a hell of a time expressing themselves.

"It's like I've got some kind of red warning light in the

back of my head, that tells me when to go," one man told me. "Some little look she gives me, or something she says, and the light goes on."

Another man said that for him, "I know it's over the first time I call up and she says she's already made some plans for the weekend for us. Suddenly it's panic city around here."

Men like these noble specimens suffer from the overwhelming fear that you're becoming much more involved than they are, that where they see a pleasant enough, but casual liaison, you see a grand and lasting passion, that what they regard as a diversion, you regard as "till death do you part." It makes very little difference what you *actually* think or feel; even if you shout from the rooftops that you, too, are only in this for the short run, they aren't likely to believe you. They'll just chalk up such protestations to your feminine wiles, or if not that, to a total repression of your *true* subconscious desires—which they, of course, believe they fully comprehend, and much better than you'll ever be able to. It's yet another of those "no-win" predicaments—tell him you love him and he's off like a shot, tell him you don't and he smiles indulgently, knowing you do, and takes off, anyway.

It sounds, I'll admit, like the ultimate in conceit, the man who believes himself to be, no matter how hard he tries to keep it in check, fatally irresistible. And in some cases, that's all that it is. In others, however, it's a thin disguise for a real feeling of inadequacy—I think that many of these men disappear when they do as a means of keeping their illusions alive. By disappearing before you've had a chance to, they can go on imagining themselves the great lover forever; they can envision you sitting tearful by the phone, waiting desperately for them to get in touch again. They can carefully cultivate, for as long as they like, the myth of themselves as the wandering heartbreaker, the Byronic loner inexorably destined, by his own magnetism, to create a wake of grieving women behind him. Preserving the illusion may leave such a man with a lot more solitary nights than absolutely necessary, but the illusion itself may indeed be his favorite company.

Sometimes, however, what men fear most of all is not *your* growing attachment, but their own. Sometimes it's because they've just been burned by a nasty break-up or a painful divorce, as was the case with my publishing friend Gerald. After five years of living together, he and his girlfriend had decided, finally, to separate. "When I went back out on the dating scene for the first time after all those years of monogamy, I think I may have gone a little crazy, and acted not so nicely a lot of the time. One thing that was really bizarre about it all was that even though I was lonely a lot of the time I would find myself dropping a woman the minute I caught myself thinking about her too much, or getting too enamored of her. Having just seen, first-hand, all the agonies of breaking up and the aftermath of a relationship, I was incredibly leery of getting involved again too soon. The minute I found myself feeling that way, like I'd like to be more deeply involved with someone, I'd stop calling her. I think, in a way, I didn't trust myself for awhile there—I figured I was much too needy for my own good."

Even without the added impetus of a recent heartache, men are often extraordinarily ambivalent about growing too close to someone. For many, it's tantamount to a confession of weakness, or dependence. A man, they feel, ought to stand alone, on his own two feet; consequently, the moment they discover themselves leaning a few degrees in anyone's direction, they pull up short. It's a scary business, loving someone—you're no longer completely in control of your own emotions, or, for that matter, your life. And while anyone, male or female, can fear that loss of control, men can experience a sort of double-whammy here, because their personal notion of masculinity may also be tied up with ideas of independence and stoic self-sufficiency. On two separate counts, needing someone may lead to obscure psychic repercussions, and unexplained behavior . . . like not calling back.

As can, finally, such dubious old notions as "love at first sight." How in the world, you may ask, can a harmless old saw like that cause any trouble, even to the perpetually perturbed male psyche? In a roundabout sort of way, I think it can lead us all—again, men and women alike—a little bit astray, if we let it. By subscribing to the tempting notion that love comes as a kind of *fait accompli,* a sudden and revelatory bolt from on high, something no sooner seen than done, we get to thinking that anytime it *doesn't* happen that way, anytime we haven't fallen head over heels after one or two dates at most, something must be fundamentally, and irremediably, wrong. If we blindly believe that the course of true love must always run smooth and straight right from the start, then the very first bump in the road is likely to send us careening off into another direction altogether. By this reasoning, why ever work at improving a relationship? If it needs work, then it's already a lost cause. With the vast pool of potential new partners out there, and the relative ease with which new ones are acquired, sometimes I think we've lost the knack of fine-tuning our affairs, along with the desire to try. Nor are we accustomed any longer to living with the consequences of our rash, irresponsible, or unkind actions; there are answering machines now to ward off all reminders of it. The man who never makes the call he promised, who chooses instead to vanish in a puff of smoke, can reincarnate himself—indeed, reinvent himself—over and over and over again, in an endless succession of new romances. The only danger is that somewhere along the line, in the course of a thousand different disappearances and transformations, he may get caught in a sort of spiritual limbo, and might no longer remember, or very much like, the man he was way back there in the first place.

Part III

The Rites - and Wrongs - of Love

Two for the Seesaw

Love is like a seesaw. This astonishing _aperçu,_ so simple and yet so complex, hit me in all its glorious profundity one idle Saturday afternoon, as I was strolling past a playground in Central Park. I was dwelling on the dismal state of my social life at the time, and secretly hoping that some sensitive woman riding by on a bicycle would telepathically tune in to my thoughts, note my tortured but amiable appearance, and beg me to join her for an intimate dinner at her apartment that night. In all the years that I've employed this method (for which I hope to receive a patent soon) I must confess that it hasn't worked even once. But what was it my high school coach used to say? A quitter never wins?

While waiting for my bicycle-riding mind reader to appear and spirit me away, I had stopped to buy an Italian ice at the entrance to the playground, and it was then that my epiphany about the seesaw struck. A little girl was being kept happily suspended high in the air by a blond boy who was leaning way back and struggling to hold his end of the beam on the ground. When he leaned forward a bit, the other end dropped, and for a moment the two of them were delicately balanced, laughing, in mid-air, their feet dangling a few inches above the ground. Now that, I thought, is the way most things—but particularly love—should be: two people working closely together to give each other joy, and more importantly, working _equally._ Because even love—sweet, simple, biodegradable love—takes some effort from both parties. A second later, the little boy on the seesaw abruptly abandoned ship and sent his playmate thumping to the tanbark.

And that, I thought, is the way it usually _is._

In nearly every relationship I know of, and certainly every one that I've been involved in, there was one person who loved more, who gave more, who worked harder to keep his partner happily aloft on the seesaw of love. That's not to say that the other person was necessarily selfish or egocentric; it was simply that the relationship had assumed that shape, had fallen into that pattern. I myself have played both roles at different times with different people, and in my mind I carry on an endless debate as to which part, the lover or the loved, I'm more comfortable in. Each has its advantages, each has its drawbacks, and two back-to-back romances, a couple of years ago, rather neatly pointed up the distinctions to me.

In the first, I was most definitely the lover, although it was only in retrospect that I realized to what an extent. From the very first moment I laid eyes on Alice, across the onion dip at a party, I was totally enraptured. Up until then, I'd been convinced I was most vulnerable to icy blondes, but suddenly I couldn't imagine anyone more alluring than this small, blue-eyed brunette. Did you ever know someone like that, someone who filled you with desire in virtually any situation, under any circumstances? I thought she was sexy when she ate a bowl of cereal, when she brushed her teeth, when she sprawled on the floor doing her exercises, or when she stood on a chair to change a lightbulb. I thought she was sexy in pink jumbo hair curlers or the avocado face mask she'd occasionally whip up. Admittedly, this kind of unrelenting passion could have proved a problem for her; in fact, I know that it did. Since I was constantly pursuing her, she was, as logic would dictate, the pursued. And even though she might not have wanted to run, I think she realized that unless she did, neither one of us would ever get anything done. At the time, that would have been fine with me; it was not, however, fine for the relationship.

Alice, of course, grew to be fairly accustomed to my constant attentions, and began to take them, not surprisingly, a bit for granted; and I eventually started to wonder if, in the absence of my ardent pursuit, the relationship would really work at all. What I found out was, it wouldn't. When I cooled off, so did the romance. The pattern had already been set, and in this instance it was just about impossible to alter.

Even after my affair with Alice had finally collapsed, I still didn't entirely understand why it had. But several months later, after I'd started seeing a woman named Barbara, I picked up a pretty big clue. I was on my way to the kitchen, Barbara was on her way to the living room, and as we passed in the hallway, Barbara stopped for a hug and a quick smooch (always a good idea in my book). The embrace, however, wasn't as brief as I'd expected it to be; Barbara hung on, and I finally had to be the one to gently disengage myself. I had no idea how to manage it tactfully, and I felt very strange unwrapping her arms from my waist. It was just after I did, though, that something occurred to me: In all the time I'd gone out with Alice, I had never once been in this position. I had never had to fend off an advance. I had always been the one clinging, long after she was ready to continue on to the kitchen, or wherever. With Barbara, it was different, because much as I liked her, I wasn't madly in love; with her, I'd assumed the role of the loved, not the lover. This time I was the one on the high end of the teeter-totter, effortlessly enjoying the ride.

But *was* I really enjoying it? At that particular moment, entangled in the hallway, no. Being the loved one does have its advantages—who doesn't like to absorb a little adulation from time to time?—but it also carries more than its share of responsibilities. You are the guardian of your lover's feelings; in a way, you are a captive of them, because one false move and you may inflict an irreparable hurt. It's at once a flattering spot to be in, and a touchy one.

Being the lover is equally precarious. On the one hand, what can surpass the joy and the excitement of feeling wildly in love with someone? But on the other, what can match the pain of love that goes unrequited? Even in those lucky instances where it *is* returned, it often happens that the love coming back at you is a lot less intense, less demanding, than your own. And that's the natural breeding ground for such unpleasant stuff as insecurity, self-doubt, and fits of jealousy.

If I've just managed to make falling in love sound like yet another of those no-win propositions, I really didn't mean to; I was only brooding on some of the relative risks and rewards involved in getting involved. On the whole, whether you're the lover or the loved, it's still better to be *in* a relationship than out of one. And anyway, the roles are neither mutually exclusive, nor irreversible; everyone is a little of each, lover and loved, and in a healthy relationship, the proportions can change at any time. Some people do, in fact, have a decided preference for one role or the other—and if you care to review your own romantic history (the next time you have a week or two to spare) you might discover a pattern there that you hadn't seen before.

As for me, I've spent most of my life quite contentedly in the part of the happy hunter, the lover who lavishes his affections and attentions on the apple of his eye. Sometimes, I'm afraid, I've probably overdone it. But today, as I am a somewhat older, possibly wiser, and certainly wearier man, I'm growing to appreciate, more and more, the unique pleasures of being the loved one, too, of just hanging up there on the high end of the seesaw and watching the world go by.

But be sure to ask me again next week, when, over another bowl of onion dip, I've spotted my next great passion.

There I go again, sounding like a spoilsport, quibbling over who loves whom more, as if love were something to be divided with surgical precision, rather than the wonderful, unifying, _sharing_ experience that it is. Falling in love is a time for celebration, for popping champagne corks, dancing in fountains, leafing through Frederick's of Hollywood catalogues together. Falling in love means facing the world with a united front, lending each other support and affection, buying pizzas by the pie rather than the slice. Falling in love means no more lonely nights watching _Twilight Zone_ reruns, no more frantic Saturday morning calls to friends to line up something to do for that evening, no more Club Med vacations. Love is truth, love is beauty, love is a relief.

Love is also perishable—especially when it first blossoms. In all the heady excitement of those early days, it's easy to knock it off before you know it, just by committing one of a handful of minor boo-boos. Despite what the philosopher Segal once wrote, love _doesn't_ mean never having to say you're sorry (I never really knew what he meant by that, anyway)—but it does mean being on the lookout for the little hurts unwittingly inflicted, the hopes too rapidly built, and the intimacy too soon presumed upon. It means, at first, tiptoeing around a few of the well-concealed traps.

"_What_ a relief," my friend Angie said to me, in the distinctive Georgia drawl that nine years among us Yankees still hasn't made a dent in. "I don't have to play all those silly old games anymore, and watch my mouth every minute to see that nothing slips out except what's supposed to. With Jack, I can completely be myself. I can let my hair down, and say whatever's on my mind. I don't have to worry about all those masks and rituals and games anymore. I can't _tell_ you how good it feels."

"A toast then," I suggested, "to the many-splendored Jack." We clinked our glasses together. "How long have you been going out?"

"Two weeks."

I stared resolutely into my glass, lest she detect any surprise in my eyes. Two weeks, and they were already baring their souls? Two weeks, and all the games were over with, all the masks dropped, all the secrets revealed? What were they going to do for the rest of the month, I wondered? Play Parcheesi?

"Next Friday we're going away together, on a vacation," she said, as if reading my mind. "Ten days in a tiny little rented cottage, right on the water, in Runaway Bay, Jamaica. Now what do you think of that?" she said smiling.

I think you're asking for trouble, I thought, though I said, "You think there's room in that cottage for a houseboy?"

"No-o-o," she drawled, running one manicured finger down my cheek, "I don't think so. This little cottage is just big enough for two."

"Well, then, bon voyage," I said, raising my glass again, "and good luck." How much I meant that, she'd never know.

Now I'm not saying that a deep and meaningful love can't spring up virtually overnight, or that Angie and Jack were heading for a surefire disaster in their little cottage by the sea. But I am suggesting—just *suggesting*—that the rapture of new love can make us forget for awhile how things normally work, how people behave, how *we* behave. A lot of things look different now—rosier, nicer, from our complexion to our prospects—so we forget some of what we used to know of life, and some of what we used to expect from it.

Like Angie, who'd had quite a long dry spell before meeting Jack, it's easy to go a little overboard at the first sign of the drought letting up. Suddenly, all those tender emotions you've been bottling up inside you have a place to go again, suddenly you don't feel so alone in the world, suddenly you feel you can let the facades fall and be yourself at last. The problem is, other people are like computers—highly developed and complex, but if you feed them too much of your personal information too fast, they break down. They just aren't able to absorb and process all that data that rapidly; Jack, for instance, I thought was liable to suffer a sudden overload and blow a fuse.

It isn't only a question of quantity, either; it's the quality, too, of the information you're asking another person to understand, and share. I once had a lunch date with a woman I hardly knew, who proceeded to fill me in on everything from her transference problem with her psychiatrist to her abortion the previous summer. These were not things I needed, or wanted, to know at that particular time; in the context of a serious and loving relationship, they would naturally have come up at some point, but this wasn't that point yet. Over hamburger platters, between two people who were barely acquainted, such bulletins seemed horrifically mistimed.

Not that I'm unaware of how strong and ungovernable that urge can sometimes be to just *unstopper* yourself; I've made the very same mistake myself. After my break-up with Alice, I found myself inundating a woman I had gone out with exactly twice with the whole, unedited, uncensored, unending account of my life, from my earliest recollections of the bassinet and strained applesauce, to the argument I'd had that morning with one of my editors. It was only the look of glassy-eyed stupefaction that I suddenly noticed creeping across her features that finally brought me up short and made me realize what I was doing. I was still missing so much the closeness and confidentiality that I'd had with Alice that I was trying desperately, recklessly, impossibly to recreate it here, in record time, with someone I hardly knew. I was trying to whip up intimacy, using an instant recipe. And it simply can't be done.

Nor will resorting to "total honesty" do the trick. I remember a friend of mine in college, a guy named Daniel, who even to this day remains one of the last "Woodstock, let it all hang out, do your own thing" holdouts; he once confided to me his method for beginning any relationship. "I sit down with her, so we're facing each other, on the floor, and I take her hands between mine, and I just tell her *everything*, everything she needs to know about where I'm coming from. I don't leave out anything—especially the women I've already been with. I think it's especially important she know that—I'm not ashamed of making love to any of the women I've made love to, and I guess I really want her to share that feeling I have about it."

Need I mention that even though Daniel was a friend of mine, I didn't buy his argument for a minute? As far as I could see, he wasn't taking a '60s openness and honesty trip, but a thinly disguised ego trip of definitely pre-'60s vintage and dimension. But that notion of honesty—of its efficacy and unquestioned virtue—seems to be a legacy many of us have inherited, without being aware that it comes equipped with its very own curse. In the abstract, honesty, of course, is all well and good—we all like to get the right change when we go to the store, we all expect our friends not to deceive us. But in a relationship, particularly a budding one, honesty, and its attendant revealing of the self, ought to be done *gradually*. That's not to say duplicity or cunning are called for; it's just to suggest that the clues to who you are ought to be parceled out one at a time, and not spilled haphazardly, all at once, across the table.

I doubt, for example, if Daniel's girlfriends gained anything whatsoever from the lengthy recitation of his previous amours. But that's a drastic case. Most of us might be inclined to share some secret wishes, fond hopes, unresolved fears; we might even be anxious to get over the early steps of courtship, or seduction, or lovemaking. But what we can wind up doing, in our great hurry to uncover everything from our dreams to our bodies, is kill all the mystery that love should revel in. Before you can say "I have an unresolved Electra complex, a freezer full of frozen Mars bars, and an erogenous zone behind my right ear," half the fun of the whole "falling in love" experience can be gone. And don't forget, anything you say *can*, and possibly will, come back to haunt you later, just when you least expect it.

For Angie, I'm sorry to say (and I do mean that, I'm *not* gloating), the hauntings came very soon indeed; in fact, she and Jack decided to cut their vacation short by two days. "The weather wasn't so great, so we both agreed to save some money and fly back early, but we both knew that wasn't the real reason," she told me later. "I guess it was all a case of too much, too soon. And too close! That cottage must have been six feet square. In any case, I made the fatal mistake at one point of saying *something*, I don't even remember what, about his ex-wife, and ka-boom! I mean, he'd been going on about her morning, noon, and night, about what'd gone wrong in their relationship and all, and then I just made some harmless little old observation and *bang*, it was World War Three in there! It took me all afternoon to patch that one up, but by the time I had," she said, leaving a long pause, "I think I was on his ex-wife's side."

Friends and Lovers

Try taking a poll sometime—ask people what ingredients they think are necessary to make a sound, successful relationship, and see what they say. "Mutual passion" you'll probably hear. And "similar values." Someone will surely volunteer that "it's just plain chemistry." Someone else will suggest the importance of a "good sense of humor" in keeping things rolling smoothly. And not a one of them would be wrong—all those things are extraordinarily important in a relationship. But so is one other thing that is seldom really noticed, and certainly never given its due—and that is friends.

All too often, our friends are the first thing thoughtlessly chucked overboard as soon as a new romance begins. Suddenly we're so wrapped up in our new lover that we no longer have the time, the energy or the interest to pursue our previous pastimes, or keep up with our old companions. Our universe becomes more closely circumscribed, and our friends frequently get left outside that circle. They start to seem vaguely superfluous, now that we have this soul-mate in whom we believe that we can utterly confide, and in no time at all, we've allowed the old ties of friendship to sag, the old bonds to slacken. And that, I think, can ultimately spell trouble for even the most solid romantic involvement.

"This is probably going to sound fairly strange," volunteered my friend Ralph, after some subtle prompting from me, "but I think a lot of what went wrong between Sue and me was due to just that, the fact that she didn't have any friends to speak of. She'd always been a loner, and a very private sort of person," he explained, "and after we moved in together, she seemed to let the few good friends she had sort of slide. I was suddenly her sole and total confidant, the one and only person she'd turn to for advice and comfort and just about anything else she needed. At first, I was not only perfectly glad to do it—I mean, I *was* in love with her—but I think I was also very flattered in a way. It made me feel very strong, very important, very *masculine*. If she was having a bad day at work, she'd call me at my office; if she had one of her frequent battles with her mother, I'd calm her down when I got home and help her forget about it. But as time went by, and I was *always* the one she turned to for anything and everything, I started to feel, I don't know, *overwhelmed,* I guess. It was as if I were a doctor on call 24 hours a day, every day. I started to feel like I was trying to handle a couple of different jobs at once, and I was having trouble juggling all the work and responsibility."

Ralph's "jobs" analogy struck me at the time as being exactly right—he *was* trying to do two jobs at once. He was trying to be Sue's lover—which is one job—and he was also being asked to take the place of her friends, which is another.

No matter how strong and loving a relationship is, it shouldn't be expected, all by itself, to satisfy *all* of our emotional needs, or to absorb *all* of the turmoil in our everyday lives. *No* relationship is strong enough for that. Nor is any one person so equipped. There are some duties, and some assistance, that only good friends can provide.

Aside from the obvious pleasures they afford us, friends can also serve as a very useful escape valve, a way to let off some of the steam and siphon off some of the pressures that otherwise we'd have no alternative but to drag home, in all their pent-up glory, to our innocent sweetheart. Instead of bursting through the door ranting and raving, we can calmly call a friend, at five o'clock sharp, and arrange to meet for a drink. And then we can do some ranting and raving *before* going home. Don't worry, either, about imposing on your friend for this service—the time will surely come when she'll call upon you to return the favor.

By using our friends for their obvious therapeutic value, we can spare our lover, from time to time, the full brunt of our daily woe. And frankly, we can *say* things we probably wouldn't be able to otherwise. There are some things that you can talk about only to a good friend, some subjects you can discuss only with him or her—such as your love life, for instance. If you want some objectivity, you can't very well go to your lover. Half the time it isn't even necessary to hear what your friend has to say in response to your remarks—it's enough to have just opened up to her, and to have heard your own words. Sometimes we don't really know what we're thinking until we've actually said it, and sometimes it's only a friend, someone close to us but not *too* close, that we can say it to. Just listening to ourselves, talking to someone we respect and care for, is often all we need to find the answers we were looking for.

Another interesting thing about friends is that they make

us more interesting. In my own vast experience of life, I have discovered that the people I most enjoy are the people who themselves most enjoy other people. (Shall I run that one by one more time?) People who have a wide and interesting circle of friends are more entertaining and pleasant to be with; they have more to say, and generally say it better. Lovers who hermetically seal themselves off from other people, who try to find in each other all that they once found in a variety of friends, can wind up going stir crazy together. Without the friendships that helped them to be the vital, vibrant people they were when they first fell in love, they can soon find themselves growing bored with each other. Sustaining a relationship in isolation is like trying to preserve a rare flower in an air-tight container—if it's not allowed to breathe, it will fast wither away.

Finally, one of the truly inestimable benefits of friends, compared to lovers, is their constancy. Romances have a well-chronicled tendency to fizzle, while friendships, if carefully nurtured, can go on forever. With each new lover, we change a little, too, become more of one thing or less of another, to adapt ourselves to the relationship. But with our friends, happily, we can always be the same person we have always been, the person we were before falling *in* love, the person we will be should we ever fall *out*. And it's at times like that, especially, that our friends can come in awfully handy.

Nightowls and Earlybirds

According to a study I once read, one of the major signs that a relationship _isn't_ going to work out shows up the very first time you sleep together. And I'm not even talking about sex here—I'm talking about actually _sleeping_ together, zonking out, sawing wood, snoozing. If you believe this study—and personally, I'm withholding judgment—the single greatest cause of conflict and discord between a man and a woman, the real root of a thousand other problems and complaints, is the pairing of a confirmed nightowl with a devoted earlybird. When sleep patterns conflict—according to the study—even love won't be able to keep the nest harmonious in the long run.

It seems to be more than a question of mere timetables— the nightowl and the earlybird seem to be quite distinct character types, with a whole host of related personality traits and inclinations. While the nightowl, for instance, is likely to suggest going to a midnight showing of _The Rocky Horror Picture Show_ and sleeping late the next day, the earlybird will be more inclined to hit the hay early (they use expressions like that) and rise at dawn to shop at the farmer's market. The nightowl will want to offer a champagne toast to the sunrise, still wearing evening clothes, while the earlybird will prefer to do it in jogging shorts, with a glass of fresh-squeezed orange juice. Like a vampire, the nightowl will only start feeling his oats when the sun sinks slowly below the horizon; the earlybird will be fading fast by that time. Clearly, there are some substantial grounds for friction, if not open warfare, here.

The reason that I'm withholding final judgment on that study is that Robin and I, just for instance, were as hopeless a mismatch on this score as you could ever hope to find. In my family, people had to set alarm clocks in order to be up in time to watch the evening news, and we didn't really start to hit our stride until the _Tonight Show_ came on. The nightly Scrabble tournament didn't get underway until the _Late Late Show,_ and we'd only straggle off to bed, countless sandwiches and sundaes later, after listening to the national anthem on two or three different stations. Even as an infant, I was purposely kept awake way past the normal bedtime so I wouldn't start crying for my morning bottle until a relatively civilized hour. What hope of change can there be, I wonder, for someone so raised, someone who associates the dead of night with family love, warmth, frivolity, and Scrabble?

Robin, sad to say, was raised in the country, on a strict Protestant ethic, and for her it was a struggle to stay up much past 11 P.M. For her, the noisy grumbling of the garbage trucks at dawn was like a rooster crowing in the barnyard, and she had to pin her own shoulders to the mattress in order, out of deference to me, to stay in bed another minute. Sometimes I tried to help her, by wrapping one arm around her throat.

There was also a problem of sleeping *styles* involved. Like most earlybirds—hard-working, optimistic, productive sorts—Robin fell asleep the moment her head hit the pillow, as if she had been suddenly bludgeoned from behind with a heavy, blunt instrument. The position she started out in was the position she would maintain, totally unaltered, for hours at a stretch; her breathing was always low and regular. The first time we spent the night together, I was sure she'd died in her sleep. In fact, at one point, hovering over her in the dark, I became so alarmed that I gently shook her shoulder.

"Are you okay?" I whispered.

"Mmmm?"

"I was just checking to see if you were okay."

"What?" she mumbled, assuming the thinnest sliver of consciousness.

"Nothing—go back to sleep." But she already had.

What about *me*? How do *I* sleep? For me, sleep is a train perpetually pulling out of the station just as I race down the platform to catch it. Its schedule is unposted and erratic, and even when I do manage to get on board, it makes frequent stops all night long. I get up to open the window, to close the window, to get a glass of water, to get rid of a glass of water; I toss and turn like a whirling dervish, pulling out the covers, pounding my pillows. Making my bed the next day means more than straightening the blankets; it usually entails hammering the frame back together.

Could this relationship be saved? The experts who compiled that study would surely have said "forget it." But I just regarded that as a challenge, and Robin and I sedulously went about meeting it. On weekends, we each managed to stagger our respective schedules by a couple of hours, so that we got up and went to bed at *almost* the same times. And at other times, I learned to creep around on my tiptoes—after three weeks, I was ready for the Bolshoi—and to listen to my records on headphones with a 30-foot cord. Robin learned to lollygag in bed for an extra hour or two, until I had become barely functional and could, with her tender assistance, dip my entire head in a pot of strong, black coffee.

What's more, we even discovered some distinct advantages to being so totally out of sync. Robin was always up in time to get the freshest and fattest croissants from the little bakery on the corner, and I could tell her anything she ever needed to know about the great old movies that go on at 2 A.M. We never had to fight for the bathroom, or the morning paper, and we frequently used each other as a convenient excuse: "I'm so sorry we can't stay to see more of your slides of Tibet, but Robin, I'm afraid, is all tuckered out"; or, "Gee, we'd really have liked to join your sunrise meditation circle, but you know Robert. . . ."

So if you're currently going out with someone whose time-table is the exact reverse of your own, take heart—who says the studies always have to be right?

Addendum: The Great Pajama Puzzle

But before we leave, for the moment, the subject of bedding down, there is one other trivial but persistent matter I'd like to touch on. It's probably going to seem odd that I bring it up at all, but it's just something I'd like to know, one way or the other, once and for all. My question, simply put, is this: Am I, or am I not, the last, living American male to wear pajamas?

I know that when I get department store catalogues in the mail, they always have at least a page or two of pajama fashions; I know that when I walk through those same stores, there is always a counter somewhere displaying the pajamas I saw in the catalogue. I know that the stores wouldn't be devoting any space to pajamas if *someone* weren't buying them, and yet, everytime I've begun a relationship with a woman, and presented myself in the bedroom doorway wearing a pair, I have been greeted with hoots, hollers, muffled laughter, screams, or just plain astonishment.

Case in point: the first time I spent the night with Robin, and emerged from the bathroom in a brand-new pair of navy blue cotton pajamas, she asked incredulously, from under the covers, "*What* are you wearing?"

"You like 'em?" I said, turning to model the billowing trousers and tunic top. "Kind of a Cossack flair, don't you think?"

Judging from her silence, she didn't.

"Why, what are you wearing under there?" I asked.

"Nothing," she said matter-of-factly, as if it were the only possible reply.

Thoroughly humiliated, I replaced my new blue pajamas in the bottom drawer of my dresser, where I keep half a dozen other pairs, and slept instead as I imagine Clark Gable always did. And all night long, to be perfectly honest, I felt cold, and, well . . . naked.

Extrapolating from Robin's reaction, and the reactions of a few other women on previous occasions, I figured I must be the only guy in the U.S. still wearing p.j.'s. So just to check, I asked a few of my male friends about it.

"Are you kidding?" said Larry. "You mean the kind with the little feet on them, and the drawbridge in the rear?"

"Of course not," I said, struggling to retain my dispassionate-interviewer tone. "I mean grown-up pajamas, *sans* feet or drawbridge."

"Not since I was old enough to sleep with my bedroom door closed. Can you *imagine*," he said, chuckling, "the kind of wimp who would wear pajamas past puberty?"

"Yeah," I said, laughing with him, "imagine what a wimp the guy would have to be." Then I quickly changed the subject.

Later, when I asked Bert and Peter, they replied pretty much the way Larry had. Phil the banker admitted to sleeping in a pair of striped boxer shorts: "But not if I have someone over," he added. "I'd feel kind of foolish, I think." Ralph said he owned two or three pairs of pajamas—Christmas gifts from his mother—"but the only time I ever unwrapped any and wore them was when I was sick in bed with the flu for a week. Otherwise, the most I ever sleep in is an old pair of jogging shorts I own."

"But what about the women in your life? What do they generally sleep in?"

After leaving a suitably long pause, as if to review the many women involved, he said, "It really varies, anything from the buff to a long flannel nightie. And to tell you the truth, I kind of prefer it when they do wear something—it adds a little mystery, and it gives you something to take off."

Larry concurred with this, adding, however, that "one of the sexiest things I ever saw a woman sleep in was just a long, white, man's T-shirt, one of those ribbed ones, that came down just as far as it had to, and not an inch further."

"Was it one of yours?" I asked.

"No, I don't wear T-shirts, either."

"Also too wimpy?"

"Yep."

So—if I am to believe Larry, Ralph, Phil, et al.—and I have no real reason to doubt them, I guess—then men *don't* wear pajamas these days (and probably not T-shirts, either). The reactions I have seen to my own p.j.'s only confirm it. But tell me, honestly, does the man you turn in with ever wear pajamas to bed? Would you write him off as a hopeless nerd if he did? (Careful how you answer this one.)

And then, answer me one more—if none of these guys ever wears pajamas, then why on earth do manufacturers keep making them, catalogues keep showing them, and stores keep selling them? Am I supporting an entire industry single-handedly? If so, I think I'm going to start asking for a discount. And *longer bottoms*.

Grappling with the Green-Eyed Monster

Normally, my friend Mike is the kind of guy who can wear out your eardrums in under an hour. I've always thought it was a pity he had no interest in politics, because if anyone was ever born to filibuster, it was Mike. That's why it was such a shock to me the last time I saw him. We were standing in that endless line for free tickets to Shakespeare in the Park, and I suddenly noticed, to my astonishment, that a silence had fallen between us. Mike was staring absently down at his sneakers, and I was eavesdropping on the couple behind us who, apparently used to these lines, were rummaging around in a picnic basket they'd brought along. "Didn't you pack any of those juicy little cherry tomatoes?" he was complaining. "They're right there, under the quiche," she said. "But would you please not eat everything now? That stuff's supposed to last all night."

After another few minutes of listening in on my neighbors, and occasionally trading a desultory remark with Mike, I finally decided to take the bull by the horns and see what was up. "Is there, pray tell, something that buggeth thee?" I asked him. "Thou art uncommon quiet."

Mike smiled, a little, and rubbed his shoe in the dirt. "Yeah, sorry. I had a pretty bad night with Jan last night, and I just can't seem to shake it."

"That's funny," I said. "I thought you broke up with Jan a couple of weeks ago."

"Yeah, well, it's not that easy. We did break up, I guess, but neither one of us particularly wants to notify the whole world about it yet. So we wound up going to this dinner party that a very rich friend of mine, a guy named Austin, had invited us to awhile back. It was a _big_ mistake."

"Bad party?"

"No, the party itself was okay; in fact, it was very impressive—silver candlesticks, great wine, a table about as long as a cabin cruiser. There were ten guests, and we were all seated in what I gather is the continental style, with all the couples separated. That's where the trouble started. Jan wound up at one end of the table, sitting next to a debonair British businessman—there _alone_—and I wound up at the other end of the table, next to the suburban mother of six children. I had to sit there listening to one story after another about little Hughie's braces, or little Louie's report card, or little Dewey's diaper rash, while Jan and the businessman were hitting it off, right before my very eyes, at the far end of the table."

"What do you mean, hitting it off?"

"I mean all that touchy-feely stuff. Every time Jan wanted to say something, I'd see her touch his arm and he'd immediately lean in close enough to breathe the same oxygen, and then I'd see them laugh together at whatever they'd just said. A couple of times—and this is what really drove me crazy—I saw him whispering something to her, with his face brushing her hair, and she'd sort of blush or smile, and look at him. It was all I could do not to jump up on my chair and holler 'What the hell are you two talking about down there?'"

"Methinks thou hast been bitten by the green-eyed monster."

"You haven't heard the half of it yet."

"Take your time—we've got at least another half-hour on line."

"When everybody'd finally finished dinner, Austin suggests we all go into the living room for after-dinner drinks. Only guess who doesn't make it that far? We're all sitting around having brandy or crème de menthe or what have you, very civilized, very posh, only Jan and Mr. Savile Row, as I had fondly come to think of him, are *conspicuously* missing. It even got to where Austin started to get a little embarrassed for my sake, and wondered out loud if they were ever planning to leave the dinner table."

"Did they?"

"Just barely. The party was already starting to break up, when Jan and Savile finally moseyed into the living room to join the rest of us. I thanked Austin for the *lovely* evening, and started to hustle Jan out of there, but Savvy was just too fast for me. 'Going uptown, are you?' in that bloody English accent. 'Mind if I share your cab?' Damn straight I minded, but what the hell could I say?"

"Sorry, old chap, but I do mind."

"Jesus, do I wish I had. Instead, I ended up sitting in the back of the cab with them, feeling like some kind of a third wheel, while they laughed and carried on all the way uptown."

"Hope you didn't have to pay the fare, too?"

"No," he said, with a small hint of satisfaction, "we got out first—he was staying at a hotel a few blocks further up—and I did *not* offer to split the fare with him. One thing that was really embarrassing, though, was when I got out of the cab, I guess I slammed the door pretty hard. This fat old cabbie in a T-shirt hangs one arm out the open window and hollers, 'Hey, pal, you got a problem, don't take it out on my car, okay?' Jan looks at me like I'm some kind of axe-murderer, and when we get upstairs—"

"This does *not* sound like you two have broken up, you know."

"Yeah, well, these things take time. It's gonna happen, though—it's inevitable. Anyway, we get upstairs and Jan starts taking the pins out of her hair and she says, 'I agree with the cabbie—what's your problem tonight?' and I tell you, it was just like a starting pistol had gone off. I was off and running, going on and on about how she'd humiliated me, with that boring prick with the gold cuff links, in front of Austin and his wife and everybody else. There was just no stopping me—and the really terrible thing about it was that I *knew* I was making a total fool of myself, I *knew* I was just digging my own grave that much deeper with every word I said, but I absolutely could not control it. The zenith—or nadir, I don't know what you want to call it—of my seizure came, and I still can't *believe* that I did this, when I got the Bible from the bookshelves in my study and made her *swear* on it—she's a Catholic, so I figured it might work—that she'd never go out with that jerk, under any circumstances whatsoever."

"You didn't?" I said, unable to suppress a laugh, and fortunately, Mike laughed, too.

"Yeah, I know, in the light of day, it seems pretty ridiculous, but I did do it. The Bible is still sitting on my bedside table to prove it."

"I take it she took the oath?"

"Reluctantly. I think I was so out of control she was afraid I'd literally explode on the spot if she didn't. Looking back on it, *I* think I might have, too."

"So where do things stand now?"

"They don't—they lie low. By the time we got up to go to work this morning, I was thoroughly chastened, and Jan, I think, now that the danger was over, was actually just a little bit flattered to see how insanely jealous I could get."

For the next 20 minutes or so, while inching along toward

the distant box office, Mike and I discussed in depth the metaphysical implications of his wrath, its origins, and its possible ramifications for world peace. And although it hadn't occurred to us until we actually had our printed tickets in hand, we were highly amused when we were reminded that the play we'd been waiting in line for all that time was none other than *Othello*. Mike watched the stage action that night as if he were attending a tutorial.

Personally, I didn't feel I needed any more instruction on the subject—jealousy and I have been close friends, much closer friends than I'd like in fact, for a long, long time. Which is why I could understand the lethal power of Mike's seizure the night before. When a jealous fit gets rolling, it gathers force like a South Seas typhoon, and levels everything—often including the romance that inspired it—in its path. It's as welcome as a wart, as sneaky as a pinch on a crowded subway, as green and all-consuming as a 12-foot alligator. But scrupulously democratic, too—anyone who claims he has never in his life felt the bite, or at least a nibble, is either fibbing, or a total amnesiac. Jealousy strikes even the best of us.

But it strikes us, I think, only when we're at our worst. Add to its previous attributes, opportunistic as a politician. Jealousy has a very hard time getting its teeth into a successful, confident, self-assured person; when God's in his heaven and all's right with the world, we're much more likely to just brush it aside if it turns up at all, and go briskly on about our business. There's no time then for such self-destructive, futile stuff; secure in our own self-valuation, we possess a strong natural resistance to the infection.

But let us weaken for even a moment, let our self-confidence be shaken by a missed promotion, a broken heart, an inexplicable weight gain, let us be feeling just the littlest bit unsteady on our feet and bam!—the crafty little creature has got its toe-hold. Now all it needs is an opportunity, like, say, a dinner party at which your partner pays more attention to someone else than to you, to grow and prosper. It'll batten onto such a chance like a mongoose onto a cobra.

I think my friend Mike was vulnerable that night because of his uncertain standing with Jan; although he still hasn't entirely made up his mind whether he wants to break up with her or not, he does know that he doesn't want anyone else forcing his hand, so to speak, or making the decision for him. There's a fair amount of "dog in the manger" about it, too—even if he no longer wants her, he's damned if he wants anyone else to have her. Childish, retrograde, reprehensible, and perfectly consistent with human nature.

But more than anything else, Mike was vulnerable because his own self-esteem had taken such a battering of late. I happen to know that a scholarly paper he's been submitting to several of the top journals in his field has been coming back with form rejections attached; he's not feeling particularly good about himself these days. And his troubles with Jan only reinforce all the insecurity and angst already brewing in him. In such an environment, jealousy can grow by leaps and bounds.

Though it seems impossible to believe at the time, when we're clutched by midnight visions of the one we love being clutched by someone else, jealousy has really got much less to do with anyone else—our lover, or anyone he or she may, or may not, be consorting with—than it has to do with *us*. At bottom, I think, it's really much less a fear of losing someone than it is a fear of being lose-able ourselves. We don't get jealous because our lover is such a miracle of perfection and desirability (though it's certain to feel that way); we get jealous because, at that particular moment, we're not very sure of our own virtues and appeal. Lacking confidence, we not only enlarge the qualities of others, but simultaneously diminish our own. And the greater the disparity that we start imagining there to be, the more tenacious the grasp that jealousy will have on us.

The real problem is that even being aware of all this doesn't help very much. We can list 16 separate, logical reasons why we're suddenly suffering from a mortal attack of jealousy, but we still go right on feeling it all the same. We know that it's probably all in our own head, but knowing that still doesn't help to get it out. We want desperately to be rid of it, but at the same time we can't let it alone; our thoughts keep returning, relentlessly, to the one subject that tortures us. We just can't seem to hurt ourselves enough—and that's when we have to stop and ask ourselves why. Why are we inflicting this punishment?

Usually, I think, it's part and parcel of that malfunctioning self-esteem. For the same reason that we're feeling unworthy or unlovable, we're also likely to be angry and dissatisfied with ourselves. That slight at the office, that bungled business deal, that lousy score on the examination, they not only knock the pins out from under us, they also make us furious with ourselves—and we lash out (or *inward*, to be more precise) with jealousy—an emotion that is at once satisfying self-punitive, and mercilessly unconstructive. Who knows how to flog us better than we do?

Is there a cure? A way to break the self-lacerating cycle? Moving to the Yukon won't help—jealousy will just hitch a ride on the dogsled; nor will plotting some elaborate revenge—revenge has a way of redounding on its perpetrator. What *might* work is opening up to your lover and admitting what it is you're going through and feeling. At times like this, confession is not only good for the soul—it's crucial to the health of the relationship.

"Even exploding," conceded Mike on our way back from the play that night, "made me feel a little bit better. I mean, I know how insane I sounded, but I was still glad that I'd vented at least some of my rage. If I'd just shut up about it and let it keep seething inside me, Jan would never have known what was going on, and things would probably have deteriorated even more than they did—assuming that's possible."

Admittedly, confessing to jealousy is no easy thing; it only looks like a good idea when compared to the alternative. But most of the time, owning up to the problem is half the battle; once that's done, you not only feel purged yourself, but your partner, who's no doubt been aware of the tension in the air, at last has something specific to address himself to. He can explain, apologize, issue tender reassurances; if he's eloquent and persistent enough, he may even succeed in squashing the green monster flat.

Or, in some instances, he may admit to his own complicity in creating it. "Once I did actually confront a boyfriend with the problem," says my friend Lisa. "We'd taken a share in a summer house, and after about two weekends out there, I could see the writing on the wall—he was hanging around this other guy's girlfriend a lot more than I thought he ought to be. I figured it was either get it out in the open and decide what to do about it, or go through the whole rest of the summer feeling utterly miserable.

"Anyway, one night back in the city—I figured it was best to do it away from the scene of the crime—I bolstered my courage with a couple of margaritas and told him that I wasn't enjoying our time at the house together, that all the attention he was paying to this other woman was starting to make me feel very jealous and unhappy."

"How'd he take it?"

"Blankly at first, and then, believe it or not, he started to smile, kind of sheepishly, and he said that even though he hadn't consciously planned it that way, he couldn't say he was sorry to hear it now. That, in fact, the more he thought about it, the more he realized he'd been *trying* to make me jealous, that lately he'd felt that I was taking him for granted a lot of the time, that I didn't seem as interested in having sex with him anymore, all sorts of things like that. All of a sudden, it all came tumbling out in the open, where we could talk about it. He was able to explain why he was coming on to the other woman, and I could talk about why I was so preoccupied and somewhat distant lately. Don't get me wrong—I'm not saying we solved all our problems in one fell swoop, but at least by the next weekend I was finally able to enjoy myself at the summer house for the first time."

Jealousy yields best, when it yields at all, to negotiated settlement, because in many ways it is essentially a question of rights and property. We're laying claim to another person, and his or her affections; we're demanding that he or she fulfill certain obligations, such as love and loyalty. It's when we feel that our claim is threatened, or the terms of the contract not being met, that jealousy rears its meddlesome head. What we have to do at times like that is think very hard about the basis of our relationship, and the boundaries we wish to impose upon it (boundaries we'll both have to abide by). What if he has a lunch with an old girlfriend? What if you have a drink with a man you know professionally? Surely these are not major flash points. But what if your beau and his ex decide to take in a movie that afternoon? Or you and your professional acquaintance stretch drinks into dinner? The waters instantly start to become murky—and murky water is just what jealousy loves to swim in.

Short of hiring a lawyer to draw up a contract between you, detailing every social transaction in which each of you is allowed to participate, there's not a lot you can do, other than to put your faith in your mutual respect and affection. If it comes to deciding whether any particular activity does or does not violate the implicit terms of your relationship, that's easy enough to solve, too: Just ask yourself if you'd be jealous if you found out that your partner was up to what you're up to now. If not, go right ahead; if so, tread lightly indeed.

And for what it's worth, keep in mind one final thing, something that occurs to me in respect to my friend Mike. Remember that business about the Bible, when he made Jan swear on it that she'd never "go out" (which I think might be translated as "sleep with") her English admirer? Though jealousy is, in most respects, sex-blind, affecting men and women for pretty much the same reasons, in pretty much the same ways, there does seem to me to be at least one fairly common difference: Men, I think, get most worked-up at the notion that their partner might be guilty of some sexual escapade with another man; women, though no strangers to strictly sexual jealousy, very often get even more upset at the thought that their man is becoming emotionally closer to, or confiding in, another woman. Hang me by my thumbs for saying so, but I still think it's true.

Early on in my own relationship with Alice, for instance, there was a little episode in which an old girlfriend of mine from college, passing through New York, made a brief stop at my apartment, where, well, not to put too fine a point upon it, I succumbed to carnal temptation. Later, Alice tumbled to the truth and we had the expected scene. But it was over in an hour, and even the residual rancor seemed to dissipate in a couple of days. It was almost as if, forgive me, such a lapse were only to be expected from a man, and if it didn't seem to presage a lifelong commitment to infidelity, it wasn't worth dwelling on. Alice, frankly, didn't seem to attach all that much importance to it after the initial shock.

What seemed to nettle her *more* was my wholehearted and unswerving devotion to another female friend, a woman named Jane, with whom I have had an extraordinarily close friendship for years. Alice never really said anything overt about it, but after a while I could tell she didn't want to hear about the hour-long phone conversation I'd had with Jane that afternoon, nor was she ever comfortable on the few occasions Jane met us for dinner or whatever. Part of it, I suppose, was because Alice knew what a big mouth I had, and probably suspected me of pouring out my heart to Jane whenever a problem in our relationship arose (true enough). But the rest of the difficulty was definitely a variant strain of jealousy—Alice resented the intimacy, the long history, the unique rapport, that I had with Jane. It wasn't *better,* or *more* intimate, than what I had with Alice—but it *was* different.

I won't say that an analogous situation couldn't arise in reverse, that a man couldn't find himself jealous over his girlfriend's male buddy. It can happen, sure. But if you really want to get a man's jealousy dynodes all heated up, you'd have to threaten the very core of his masculinity, the most fundamental part of his essential maleness. You'd have to put his sexual control on the line. For better or for worse, men are as much in competition with each other today as they have ever been—they compete for power, for money, for status, and of course, for women. Even today, in the year of Our Lord 1983, a man exults inside when a woman he desires consents to sleep with him; and so, too, does he fly into a rage if he feels that his exclusive sexual license to her is in jeopardy. If another man threatens to intrude on his territory, his first reaction is going to be to drag his woman back into the cave by her hair, and then sally forth with his club slung over his shoulder. (Or perhaps, if he's reasonably civilized, to make her swear on the Bible not to give herself to his rival.)

The equations just aren't the same: Possession for a man usually means *physical* possession; possession for a woman means *emotional* possession. A man's ego is most clearly threatened if he thinks his woman has given herself physically to another man. That's the greatest blow to his pride. A woman's ego is more wrapped up in the depth of the love and commitment in the relationship; it's when *that* is endangered, that she's most likely to feel the grip of the green-eyed beast. What remains true in either case is the modus operandi of the unwelcome guest, jealousy; in both sexes, it strikes at the ego, precisely where it lives. In women, it hits chiefly at the heart, at the fervent wish for trust and intimacy; in men, it's just as likely to hit below the belt. Jealousy is *not* a classy opponent, it never claimed to be. But it is, I'll grant, a formidable one.

How to Tell He Loves You If He Won't Say So

The first time, as a mature adult, that I ever burbled the words "I love you" to someone, it was done, I can safely say, without any conscious thought or premeditation. The words simply tumbled out, in an especially torrid and intense moment, and I think I was just as surprised to hear them as was Carol, the object of my passion. But once the words were out there, hanging importantly in the air between us, I wasn't at all sorry; in fact, I rather liked the way they sounded, so I tried them out a few more times. It got easier and easier as I went along. And I, released at last from that terrible male phobia, finally over the verbal hump, felt enormously proud of my grand accomplishment, and at the same time delighted to discover that I meant what I said. I truly was in love!

So for Carol, I guess, it was easy—she knew I loved her because I said so. But judging from what many women tell me, the job is often a good deal more difficult than that. Many men, true to their historical precedents, remain the classic "inarticulate beast," the strong but silent hulk who would sooner don a tutu and dance down the street than utter the fearful formula, "I love you." So how, I am often asked, is a poor girl to know when a man's in love with her? What are the signs and portents to look for? What strange behavior will he suddenly display? And is there any way at all, short of thumbscrews and the rack, to drag a tender declaration out of him?

Well, drawing on my extensive research into male psychology and conduct, I think I can honestly say, "Damned if I know." There are no surefire answers or indicators; each case, each man, is unique. Of course, I can make some suggestions. Has he, for example, started picking up his socks, splashing on the Paco Rabanne, or washing out the dishes that used to sit in the sink for weeks at a time? Does he call regularly, show up when and where he's supposed to, drop by your office unexpectedly to escort you home, or just to say hello? Has he begun to exhibit a much greater interest in your friends, your family, and most important of all, your cat, dog, or goldfish? All of these are good signs that he's at least well on his way to being in love, even if he hasn't said so yet.

Another simple ploy, suggested by the immediately preceding section of this book, is to off-handedly mention that an old boyfriend's in town and has called to ask you to lunch. An uninvolved suitor will probably take such news with perfectly good grace; he may even feel vindicated for some of *his* own recent sorties. A man in love, on the other hand, will sulk, get mad, or at some point later in the evening, clumsily contrive to mention that, as it happens, an old girlfriend of *his* has recently been in touch, too, and he was thinking of giving *her* a call. This is not to be believed, of course, but merely jotted down on your data sheet.

With many men who are slow to verbalize their feelings, women have had to reluctantly fall back on the old saw that "actions speak louder than words" (or the absence thereof); if he's tender and kind and thoughtful, they figure, then that's what really matters, and what difference does it make what he says or doesn't say? In most cases, this is a perfectly valid and operative principle. Even with Carol, for instance, the woman to whom I made my first declaration, the words themselves, nice as they were to hear, apparently came as no revelation.

"I've known since February," she coolly explained. When I pressed for details, she reminded me of a night she was driving into the city to meet me at my apartment, and because of a heavy snowstorm, arrived two and a half hours late. By the time she got there, I was frantic and furious, and proceeded to bawl her out for not having called, and for not having had the sense to abandon the plan in the first place. "When I saw you blow your top like that, which I'd never seen you do before, that's when I knew how worried you were about me, and how much you really cared." (Who said there's no such thing as feminine intuition?)

Which isn't to say it can't be wrong at times—particularly when a woman is desperately looking for reassurance of a man's feelings for her. Take my friend Betsy, for example, who for years was dating the same smarmy lawyer, named Malcolm. No, Malcolm hadn't ever said he loved her, and yes, they did seem to fight a lot, but gee, she'd say, take a look at these $500 boots he'd just bought her to make up for the way he'd treated her at the party. Or yes, they had broken up again, but Malcolm had called the very next day with round-trip tickets to St. Thomas, and how could she remain apart from a man who so clearly cared for her? Bright as she was, Betsy could never see what all of us around her saw—that

Malcolm didn't care for anyone but himself, and that all of his expensive gifts were nothing but bribes. He may not have had any love to give, but he could throw around all the money he liked.

Finally, there are some men as profligate with words as Malcolm was with dollars, and they're no more to be trusted than he was. "I love you" may have sprung to their lips five minutes after bumping into you on a bus, they may chant it like a mantra every morning, noon, and night, but chances are, they also "love" plenty of other things, too, from blueberry yogurt to the films of François Truffaut. For them, the words, and the sentiment, are as devalued as a Moonie's smile; they come too easily, with too little thought, or too *much* calculation. Saying "I love you" ought not to be treated like 100-year-old brandy, decanted only on the rarest of occasions, but neither should it be poured out as liberally as cheap rosé. If it were only said as often as it is sincerely felt, then that would be just about right. And in the meantime, if it happens that you're still waiting to hear the words, you might just check to see if he's washed his dishes, discovered cologne, or petted your cat—all good signs of the man in love. If he hollers at you for getting in late, then you know you're home free.

_____What Do Men See in Playboy, Anyway?_____

My friend Denise is getting a little worried. Two years ago, when she first started dating Ben, he was living with an old college classmate, and she just naturally assumed that the copies of _Playboy_ she occasionally found in their apartment belonged to the roomie. Then the roomie moved out, and she moved in, but the _Playboy_s kept showing up each month. Now Denise and Ben have taken a new apartment, they're engaged to be married next fall, and she's still finding new issues of _Playboy_ (and once, a _Penthouse_) tucked into the magazine rack. She doesn't know that she wants to have an actual confrontation over it—"I mean, once in awhile, I read some of the articles myself," she admits—but she does wonder why, with the woman he adores within constant reach, he still bothers to buy the magazine at all.

"On feminist grounds alone," she says, "I'm not so crazy about his buying _Playboy_. But more than that, I sometimes feel a little insulted that he should still want it, or worse yet, need it in some way. I'm almost afraid to ask him, because I don't know if I really want to know why."

Even if she did ask—which I recommended she do, at some well-chosen moment—I doubt Ben would be able to explain it very clearly. He's a first-rate lawyer, used to arguing cases in court with logic and vigor, but the reasons why men, from all stations in life, still subscribe to skin books long after the first pangs of puberty have subsided, and they've discovered what sex is really all about, are many, mysterious, and complex. Even Hugh Hefner probably doesn't know for sure.

With one group, encompassing sexual psychopaths, long-term convicts, army privates, oil-derrick crews in the North Sea, and randy 15-year-old boys, there's no need to search for elusive forces or complicated causes. They buy _Playboy_, and its much sleazier rivals, to "look at the pictures," marvel and fantasize. It's all fairly cut and dried.

But Ben hasn't been marooned in a barren waste for the past two years, he doesn't suffer from the agonies of satyriasis, and his sexual relationship with Denise, from what she tells me, is just fine. (In fact, he'd probably kill me if he knew just how much she's divulged.) For Ben, like many other mature, intelligent, and in most respects "liberated" men, the porn magazines serve a couple of different purposes (besides providing pictures to look at) and one of them, I think, is oddly sentimental.

Hard as it is to recall, there was a time, not so long ago, when every corner newsstand wasn't glutted with pornography, and when the guy inside wouldn't sell to anyone under 18. Men who are now in their late 20s, early 30s, remember those days. At that time, *Playboy* was the only known game in town, and to acquire a copy, to comb over it with your friends in the junior high locker room, was a major triumph. When I was growing up in Chicago, there was only one boy in my class, Eric Busby, who had the nerve to go in and buy one, and there was only one newsstand we knew of where the owner would look the other way. For every copy Eric bought for one of us, he pocketed a 25¢ commission. By the eighth grade, Eric could have retired comfortably for life.

The mere feel of a *Playboy*, with its heavy stapled binding, slick cover, glossy paper, was enough to start the blood racing, while the huge promise of the photos, and the fold-out within, could threaten an overactive, pubescent pituitary with sudden implosion. Those heady days are long gone, but the memory lingers still. For many men like Ben, even if they're in no way conscious of it, a copy of *Playboy* still carries a kind of residual impact from those innocent times, like listening again to the early Beatles songs, or reading through mash notes you found stuck in your three-ring notebook. *Playboy* sex, titillating as it was, was safe, remote, and utterly fantastical, too—which, in this tangled, grown-up world of commitment, contraception, and responsibility, retains a good deal of its original appeal.

So does the attitude, everywhere implicit—or explicit—in the magazine, of a male fraternity, an upscale but nevertheless macho bond, composed of such things as fine Scotch, sports cars, and state-of-the-art stereo components. After all, just because a man has a law degree, it's no guarantee that deep in the innermost recesses of his heart, he's totally confident of his masculinity. And just because he's loving, thoughtful, and decent in his daily life, that's no reason to believe he doesn't sometimes dream in his off-hours of playing Warren Beatty, of loving and leaving 'em, right, left, and center. *Playboy* and the like cater to the fantasy, at the same time that they offer a simple and eminently comfortable, "manly" world to relax in. Confronted in everyday reality with changing sex roles and independent women, with male secretaries and female execs, even some of the most progressive-thinking men—Ben, for instance—may occasionally retreat to a *Playboy* state of mind. It's not, as I tried to reassure Denise, fatal.

Nor is it any reflection on her. However fundamentally immature the whole business may be, it's not any indication of sexual restlessness, domestic dissatisfaction, or frustrated voyeurism. She doesn't have to take Ben to the doctor, she doesn't have to lock him in at night, and she doesn't have to worry about air-brushing herself. Immersed in *Playboy,* he's just reaching out, unknowingly, toward his own lost innocence, reinforcing the fragile walls of his beleaguered masculine identity, and, well, yes, "lookin' at the pictures." When he starts pasting fold-outs on the bedroom walls, that's the time to bring out the heavy guns.

Why Love Doesn't Travel Well

As suggestions go, it was a perfectly harmless one—at least on the surface of it. All Alice had said was, "I've got some vacation time coming to me. Why don't we go off somewhere together?"

She had every right to expect some enthusiasm from me. At the time, we'd been going out together for over a year, and the only bucolic escapes we'd managed were occasional weekends in the country, and one disastrous business trip to Miami Beach that I had dragged her along on, thinking we could make a vacation of sorts out of the odd free hours. It rained the whole time.

But fears of inclement weather, lost luggage, terrorist hijackings, ruinous expense, are only bits and pieces of my fundamental, hard-core, pathological vacation-phobia. For me, vacationing with a lover has proved a surefire invitation to disaster, an open call to calamity from far and wide. It has signaled the death of one relationship, and seriously jeopardized a couple of others. Today, the very mention of a vacation sends me into a sudden panic—which did not escape Alice's notice after she'd suggested we go off together.

"Thanks a lot," she said. "Can't you stand the idea of being off alone with me somewhere? Or are you just afraid to make any plans that presuppose we'll still be going out two or three weeks from now?"

Hard as I tried, I don't think I was entirely successful at convincing her those were not my problems. As far as I was concerned, our relationship was good and durable, and the *idea,* the abstract idea of being alone with her, the tropical sun beating down on our city-white faces, the palm trees swaying in the warm, ocean breeze, was awfully inviting. It was the *reality* of it, familiar to me from grim experience, that I dreaded.

In the comic strip "L'il Abner," there was a sad little character named Joe Btfsplk, over whose head, wherever he went, there followed a rain cloud; in real life, that character is me. If I were to vacation in Death Valley, my visit there would prompt ceaseless and torrential downpours. Countries with large arid tracts of land should send me a complimentary ticket, for I have only to arrive for the rains to begin. I can make the desert bloom simply by setting out my chaise longue.

But still, the real danger of vacationing, so far as I was concerned, was more subtle than that. To my mind, a lot of relationships, no matter how sound they may seem on an everyday basis, simply don't travel very well. There's just nothing like finding yourselves a couple of thousand miles from home, in a land where the two of you must rely entirely upon each other for company and conversation, to truly test the mettle of an affair. Without your daily routine to fall back on, without your things all around you to provide camouflage and diversion, you are both, as it were, stripped down to essentials. All you carry with you, aside from what you've managed to fit into your suitcase, is who you are. And sometimes that takes some serious getting used to.

"But we've been going out for months," you may say to yourself. "If we don't know each other by now, we never will." If this thought does pass through your mind, you should follow it up immediately by asking yourself this: "Does *he* really know all about *me*? Am I precisely the same person in his company as I am when I'm here at my apartment alone?" Unless you're a very rare specimen indeed, the chances are decidedly against it. When you're going out with someone, you still have plenty of time to yourself, and your own apartment as a refuge. So does he—and when you both leave the security and solitude those apartments afford, in order to be together in a foreign place, full-time, you're entering a new situation altogether.

For that reason, I think it's absolutely essential that you reach some clear understandings before even opening a travel brochure. One is that you won't necessarily be spending every second with each other, that if one of you wants to go snorkeling and the other wants to visit the horticultural gardens, you'll both go your separate ways for the afternoon and meet back at the room in time for dinner. It seems a simple enough rule, but since most of us think of vacations as a time for togetherness, we tend to regard any signs of independence, our companion's or even our own, as an indication of some brewing discontent. Back home, we certainly wouldn't put that construction on it, but on vacation, we can feel like a traitor just by asking for an hour alone.

The hidden bonus in such a policy is likely to show up at the end of the day, when you both find yourselves elated to see each other again, and brimming over with news of your personal adventures. If you'd done everything in tandem all afternoon, all you'd be able to do over dinner is swap pretty much the same bunch of anecdotes and observations, which, after a few days, gets less and less exciting. Going your separate ways, now and again, gives you both a chance to recharge and restock.

As will reaching out and meeting other people at the resort, or hotel where you're staying. Unless you're billeted at a Club Med, or one of those places that actively encourages mingling among the guests, it's sometimes difficult to meet other couples. You're often assigned to a private table in the dining room the moment you arrive, and trying to join some other people at theirs, or inviting them over to yours, can prove as intricate a procedure as hooking up with a space station in orbit. My advice is to go ahead and do it, anyway. The notion that a vacation is designed for total intimacy, and total intimacy means no other people allowed, is crazy and counterproductive; what's more intimate than going back to your room together at night to deride and ridicule the other couple you just had drinks with?

What you *don't* want to do, however, is go anywhere that summons up, for either of you, the ghosts of former affairs. There are more than enough destinations in this world, enough sunny isles, snow-capped peaks, and sights worth seeing, to provide each new relationship with its own fair share. Whatever the reason or impulse behind it, returning to a place you once visited with a previous love is not only unwise—it's unkind, too, to your current companion.

But if, after all I've said, you're still determined to chance a vacation together, start out *small*. Don't make your first expedition together a four-week, 16-country trek; make a sort of brief "trial run" first. Rent a car and drive to a country inn for a long weekend, or spend a few days together at a comfortable ski lodge within easy commuting distance of home. Do *not* sublet your apartment for the time you plan to be away; you never know when you might suddenly need it again.

Because even with all the planning in the world, with all these various caveats and precautions in mind, you still can't tell for sure how well you'll vacation together; in the end, it's all a matter of your respective "traveling dispositions," and how well they match up. With my old girlfriend Carol, for instance, her natural propensities to tidiness and punctuality were magnified enormously the moment we set off on a trip.

Her packing was a marvel of economy and ingenuity, everything neatly compartmentalized, stockings tucked in shoes, toiletries in zip-lock bags, camera already loaded and ready to go. Unfortunately, she tended to pack her emotions away just as carefully. She became aloof, a little rigid, much less spontaneous and affectionate. The trip seemed to occupy so much of her attention that there was very little left over for me.

I, on the other hand, became an impossibly romantic nuisance. While I couldn't be troubled to read a roadmap or make a reservation, I could be persuaded to get unduly amorous in every cab, elevator, bathtub, restaurant, bus, you name it. I also revealed myself to be a much more advanced case of "New York manic" than ever before imagined, driving through the Cotswolds, with no particular destination in mind, as if I were competing in the Indy 500, or fuming at the breakfast table in Bermuda when my three-minute egg took all of four minutes to prepare. Thrown into stark relief against the unhurried rhythms of the English countryside or a tropical island, I became a living, breathing indictment of the modern-day city life.

As you might have guessed, Carol's traveling disposition and mine were not very well suited to each other. But that didn't stop us from trying, over and over again, to enjoy a vacation together. The showdown came on a trip to Cape May, New Jersey, and in all honesty I can't even remember what the original quarrel was about. I just remember stomping out of our motel room (actually a couple of large rooms with a kitchenette) and out to the boardwalk. It was an unusually cold Fourth of July evening, and the fireworks display was scheduled for later that night. In high dudgeon, I walked all the way down the boardwalk, quite a fair distance, and sat down at the end on a rocky promontory where some old men were fishing. I must have sulked there in the cold ocean breeze for at least half an hour, because I remember when I got up I was totally numb in the nether regions. And suddenly I realized that unless I got back quickly, Carol and I wouldn't have time to settle our differences and watch the fireworks together. Dragging my paralyzed posterior along as best I could, I crawled back toward the motel. People were already flocking to the beach, wrapped in sweatshirts and blankets, to see the show. I was just regaining my normal stride when I spotted Carol outside a penny arcade, wearing my blue windbreaker. She must have seen me at precisely the same moment; we both stopped dead in our tracks and stared at each other. Her hands were on her hips. I held mine a few inches from my sides, right about holster level. She then did the same, and slowly, one step at a time, we approached each other, like gunfighters at high noon. When we were at a distance of about 20 paces, the first fireworks suddenly exploded over the ocean with a loud bang and crackle; we drew our imaginary pistols simultaneously and shot. She slumped against a wooden railing, and I tumbled off the boardwalk altogether and sprawled on the sand.

When she came to my side a few moments later, and cradled my head in the crook of her arm, she suggested that from now on, all things considered, for her sake and mine, perhaps we ought to consider taking separate vacations. And I, with my dying breath, said I'd certainly be willing to think about it.

Part IV

Fooling Around

___How to Seduce a Man___

At first glance, the very notion may seem a trifle odd. Seducing a man? What's there to know? You kiss him once, not even hard, and he's off to the races. Done.

Well, I won't say it can't happen that way. Much of the time, much of the male gender does operate with the same complexity as a rubber band. But just because we *sometimes* respond on a primitive and purely instinctual level doesn't mean that at other times we can't raise ourselves from the primordial ooze long enough to appreciate the subtler and finer things in life. Such as being seduced.

Seduced not in the sense of being bent, against our own will, to someone else's sexual purpose, but seduced in the sense of being artfully, creatively, imaginatively made love to. If there's one thing men secretly relish, one thing we privately revel in, it's the chance, from time to time, when nobody's looking, to be passive. To be taken. To be coddled, caressed, even (within limits) manhandled. A man seduced is a man who feels, blissfully, that for once the pressure is completely off him, that for once the course of events is beyond his control, that his only responsibility is to sit (or lie) back and tranquilly, humbly, and with ineffable gratitude, *accept*.

"You know what the best thing about it is?" said my friend Larry (after I'd asked him, of course). "It's not having to guess what the woman is thinking for once. It's not sitting around all night wondering does she want to, or doesn't she, will she or won't she, should I try or shouldn't I. When a woman is acting in an honest to goodness seductive way, the relief alone is enough to instantly lower my blood pressure by 100 points—or degrees, or whatever they measure blood pressure in."

"I should think your blood pressure would *rise* when you were being seduced."

"Well, *obviously* I get excited. I just mean that I feel much more relaxed, knowing the whole business is sort of settled beforehand, and out of my hands completely. It feels great," he concluded with a sigh. "I just wish it would happen more than once or twice a decade."

But what, you may well ask, does Larry mean when he says

"an honest to goodness seductive way"? Do you have to be a flaming redhead in stiletto heels, draped across a crushed velvet divan? Must you live in a lavish, penthouse apartment, festooned with ceiling mirrors, bead curtains, and erotic etchings? And does seducing a man mean in any way demeaning yourself, or compromising your own pleasure?

If it does, then you're doing something wrong. Seduction in my book is one of the few things in life that can be accomplished for mere pennies, by anyone with the will to try, and which yields in the end equal rewards for both the giver and the givee. If you take the time and the trouble and the care to "seduce" the lucky man in your life, the pleasure and the happiness that you give to him is bound to come back at you, then or later, with no less than trebled force. So be sure to batten down the hatches!

Arranging the Props

Absolutely key to a successful seduction, I think, is the element of surprise. Do not call a man at his office on Monday morning and say, "Hi, it's Gloria—are you free to be seduced on Wednesday night?" This is no way to get things off the ground. Just keep it simple and discreet: "I've got this terrific new recipe for something called fettucine Gianninni, and I'd love to try it out. Are you free for dinner some night this week?" Once he's said yes, that's when you can start making your plans in earnest.

On the appointed night, in the hours just before he arrives, there are any number of things you should do to set the scene. First of all, and this is terribly easy to forget, disconnect the phone; you don't want a jangling telephone to interrupt a once-in-a-lifetime moment. If you have an answering machine, so much the better; flick it on with the audio monitor *off*, so that your father's voice doesn't come suddenly booming across the room, "Gloria, honey, your mother and I are driving into the city this weekend to bring our little baby some of her favorite homemade noodle pudding. . . ."

If you're fortunate enough to live in one of those stunning, penthouse suites, then you don't have to worry so much about creating a seductive environment. But if, like most of us, you live in a more modest apartment, of less generous dimensions, commanding a view of a supermarket or areaway, you might like to enhance the romantic potential of your digs by such simple but effective means as lowering the blinds, emptying the ashtrays, or killing the fluorescent overhead light. Lighting is, in fact, one of the most crucial elements to a projected seduction—test the room with various lamps off and on to see which combination casts the most roseate glow. Don't turn off so many that on his way in he trips over the cat and impales himself on the umbrella stand, but don't leave on any more than are strictly necessary. If you can get a pink bulb or two, or even drape a red scarf over a lampshade, that's a nice touch—as, of course, are candles.

I would like to say this about candles, however—lovely and wonderful as they are, a couple of women I have known in my time have gone a little overboard on this score. I can remember a few occasions when the whole evening felt like one of those old nickelodeon films, dark and flickering and hard to follow. And I can remember another occasion when I entered a woman's apartment that looked like it was set up for some kind of ritual Black Mass, with guttering candles in flat, glass dishes all over the floor, bookshelves, windowsills, and mantelpiece. When she announced we were having chicken for dinner, I was afraid she was going to eviscerate it right there on the coffee table.

Just as subtle as the illumination should be the musical background. I say "background" because that's exactly what it should be—moody, melodic, audible but never insistent. If you happen to know his musical tastes, that's fine; if they run to country-western, plop old Willie Nelson's "Stardust" on the turntable; if he likes classical, a lush Rachmaninoff concerto will do. "But if you're gonna tell women what music to play for a night of seduction," said my friend Larry, "tell 'em *never*, under any circumstances, to play 'Bolero.'"

"Too blatant?" I said.

"Too *nerve-wracking*. Not only do I happen to hate that piece of music, but by now I think just hearing it can leave a guy impotent."

Of course, the single most mood-inspiring factor for any man, far more important than indirect lighting or a Chopin prelude, is going to be you. How you're dressed, and how you present yourself. "Aha!" you might say to yourself. "If I'm planning to stage a seduction, I'd better dress in some sensationally sexy fashion—maybe thigh-high boots and the shortest skirt I own. Or perhaps Saran Wrap, tied with bright red ribbons, and garnished with an ankle bracelet." But dressing in the most provocative manner you know is also, I think, a mistake. Not only is it a bad idea to telegraph your intentions that way the moment you open the front door—he shouldn't know that fast that a seduction is afoot—but dressing *too* sexily is likely to lead to your being *un*dressed again before you've had a chance to take his coat. Many men fall a bit short in the patience and restraint category, and the best-laid plans for an elaborate seduction can be drastically curtailed if you throw him into a frenzy of lust too soon. (Not that that's *all* bad!)

And the most *obvious* outfits aren't necessarily the ones that men find most alluring, anyway; in seduction, you want to get his senses slowly smoldering, not ignited in one burst with the first match you put to them. When I was talking to some of my male friends about what they'd find a seductive outfit, I didn't once hear anything about see-through blouses or glossy gift-wrap. One thing I did hear, and more than once, was leg-warmers.

"But I guess a woman wouldn't be wearing them indoors, huh?" commented my friend Gerald. "Well, I don't care—she ought to. Leg-warmers over a pair of tight jeans is one of the sexiest looks I know."

"I'll take some kind of a loose-fitting, diaphanous, but definitely not transparent (that's tacky) gown of some sort," said Ralph. "I had one girlfriend who used to wear these beautifully colored silk kimonos that her brother—he was in the Navy—used to send her from Japan. What I liked best about them was their wide sleeves—I could snake my hand up them and hold her by the elbow. She had terrific elbows."

Though men aren't generally thought to notice such things, a lot of my friends commented on the fabric and texture of a woman's clothing as much as on the fit or cut of it. They loved skirts and blouses that were sheer, silky, or soft to the touch. "I guess it's kind of an opposites thing again," said Larry. "My own clothes tend to be fairly heavy or rough—tweedy jackets, corduroy pants, even my ties are those knit ones. So I really appreciate the chance to run my hand around something smooth for a change. Not to mention her clothes, ha-ha."

Fragrance, too, came up frequently. Tastes ranged from the musky—"I like to feel drenched in it," said one friend—to the "light, and kind of lilac-y," according to Ralph. But they all concurred that the woman who underestimates the influence of the male nose is making a serious oversight, a view with which I, too, am in full agreement. Like a lot of men, I really enjoy a pleasant, delicate scent, but I still don't bother to slap on the aftershave or cologne unless it's a fairly special rendezvous I'm going to; I'd never do so before going to a round of business appointments, for instance. I suppose in some buried part of me I may still harbor some secret doubts about the manliness of it. So it's all the nicer to revel in a woman's perfume; Carol, I recall, kept sachets in all her clothes drawers, and sometimes before we were ready to turn in, lightly spritzed the bedsheets with an atomizer of cologne. I loved it, not only because the fragrance itself was so appealing, but because it was one more way in which sleeping with her, in her bed, was demonstrably *not* sleeping alone, on my own little pallet. I delighted in every such reminder.

The Action Begins

Finally, everything is in readiness—the lights dimmed, the music playing softly, your blouse unbuttoned to just the right level (no, maybe it's too much, maybe one more should be fastened. You fasten it. No, it was right the first time—you unbutton it again. On the other hand . . .). The doorbell rings. You lunge for the knob, yank the door open.

The United Parcel man holds a package from your mother. (Probably noodle pudding.) "Sign here, please," pointing to line 41 on the clipboard. You notice his eyes stray, you nimbly fasten another button, scratch your name on the paper, close the door. Thirty seconds later, when you've just chipped a nail getting the string off the package, the doorbell rings again. This time you handle it better; you tamp the broken nail down, undo the top button for the last time, and wait, tapping your foot gently on the carpet, until the second ring has just begun, and then open the door in one slow sweep.

"Why, Alex—what lovely flowers. Come in."

While Alex is taking in the romantic ambiance of the room, you drop his $2.95 bouquet into a vase of water. "What can I get you to drink?" you ask, cracking open the ice tray, and knowing exactly what he'll say.

"Scotch, on the rocks, please. Hey, Gloria, the place looks great tonight." Relief—you haven't gone to all this trouble for nothing.

Rule number one—resist any impulse to pour him a stiffer than usual drink. Yes, it's true that alcohol is an effective relaxant, and un-inhibitor—but it has also been proven, in clinical tests at 17 leading universities, to induce drowsiness, and in sufficient quantities, to interfere with a man's sexual drive and vigor. That's one problem you don't need tonight, so make his drink generous enough to last till you pop open the wine with dinner, but not so large that it takes two hands to lift it.

Speaking of dinner, that's rule number two—even if you happen to be an honors graduate of the Cordon Bleu school, don't go to the trouble of preparing a meal miraculously complicated or exotic. You don't want to be fretting over hot stoves and timers and saucepans just now. Prepare something that can be finished beforehand and served cold, or just heated up quickly. Also, keeping in mind the ultimate aim of the evening, make it something light and easily digested— the man who has just consumed twice his own body weight in Beef Wellington and potatoes à la Pavarotti is not likely to prove the most ardent swain a half hour later.

Frankly, what you serve is probably of less significance in most instances than how you serve it. We're all quite aware that men are getting more and more talented these days at whipping up elegant little dinners of their own, but on behalf of all my fellow incompetents, I'd just like to say that there's still a pretty fair number of us out there who wolf down our dinner while standing over the sink, where our crumbs and discarded utensils can simply be let fall. For us, the sight of a loaf of warm French bread, nestled in a wicker basket, or a shiny china plate with color-coordinated portions of meat and vegetable, can be both comforting (that's how Mother used to make up our dinner plate) and sensual. "You know that girlfriend of mine who used to wear the kimonos?" said Ralph. "She used to make these terrific little dinners for us, that we'd eat sitting on the floor on top of these huge, squishy cushions. She didn't ever cook anything all that grand—I mean, no ducks in orange sauce or anything like that—but the stuff she did make, she'd bring in in these big, round platters, divided up into half a dozen compartments. In one section, there'd be sautéed mushrooms, in another baby sausages, in another some blanched vegetables of some sort. It was sort of like a smorgasbord, I guess, but it was really a lot of fun to eat."

"I know why you liked it," I said. "What with all those different things to serve, she had to keep rolling up her sleeves and exposing her perfect elbows."

"That's weird you should say that," said Ralph. "Because that's just what I was thinking about just now. Weird."

A Perfect Kiss

The segue from dinner (and do *not* stop to do the dishes) to the post-prandial activities is nicely accomplished over a glass of brandy, or the last of the wine. Nature being what it is, in no time at all the two of you will probably find your fingers interlaced, your faces cheek to cheek, or perhaps your lips engaged in that interesting conformation commonly known as a kiss. I know that I need hardly tell you how to kiss a man, but would you be terribly insulted if, in a purely constructive spirit, I did offer a couple of small suggestions and comments?

How, for instance, do you like to *be* kissed? Do you like a guy to lunge toward you, grab you by the hair, mash your lips, splinter your teeth, root around in your mouth with his tongue like an anteater in search of his supper? No, I think not. At least not to start with. And yet, I think that there are some women laboring under the impression that that's the way *men* want to be kissed. Violently and passionately.

Well, passion is all well and good, in its place, but a kiss that leaves the recipient looking like he just escaped from a football scrimmage with the Green Bay Packers is not the best way to get things rolling. I can remember one woman, very pretty, very prim, very proper, for whom a kiss appeared to be a form of calisthenics. Every ounce of energy she had went into that initial lip-to-lip contact, her mouth wide open, wet as an ocean, insistent as a magazine salesman. When it was finally over, I'd have to towel myself off and wring out my shirt. It was a lot like kissing a St. Bernard, I figured.

I also had the nagging feeling that she was kissing that way less for her own pleasure than for what she imagined to be mine. I think she thought it certified her as a sexy, in-touch, take-charge woman. But from my point of view (behind the diving mask and wet suit) it just looked . . . saturating.

What is a good—and seductive—kiss? It's one that's passionate but restrained, firm but pliant, moist but not sloppy. It lingers, long enough to make its point, but does not attempt to set a marathon record. It employs the tongue, as a rapier not a broadsword, and sometimes the teeth, to nibble but not to chew. It tastes perhaps of wine or honey or mint, not of tobacco, Binaca, or anxiety. And it is performed, always, with the eyes closed.

"To tell you the truth," confessed Ralph, "sometimes, when I wasn't really very involved, I'd kiss with my eyes open, just to see what was going on, how involved the woman was. Until one time, I happened to kiss a woman who had her own eyes open—Jesus, I nearly jumped right out of my skin! It was like kissing a Cyclops. Since then, I've always kept my own eyes closed just because I'm afraid of what I might see."

"To give the devil her due," said my friend Mike, still not entirely over his attack of jealousy, "Jan was a grade-A kisser. She'd put one hand very lightly against the back of my head, the other flat against my chest, and she'd just kind of roam around, kissing me on the cheeks, or the eyelids, or the neck, where she knows—*knew*," he corrected himself, "I was ticklish. She had this uncanny talent for reading my nerve endings, and she always knew exactly the right place to plant the next kiss."

Knowing where to kiss isn't quite as difficult as it might seem, especially since any kiss planted with tenderness and desire is never in the *wrong* place.

The Laying On of Hands

"If I had a nickel for every time sex started out with a back rub," says Larry, "I'd have a quarter today. No, seriously, to my mind the offer of a back rub is just another way of saying, 'Do you wanna go to bed together?' How do I know this? Because of my own past experiences? Partly. Because of my profound understanding of human psychology? Partly. But most of all, I know this because I know that that's what a back rub means whenever I offer to give one."

If the lineage of the back rub could be traced on some sort of genealogical chart, I think it would be clear that its earliest antecedents include such things as wrestling on the playground, pillow fights in the dorm, dunking at the beach—any activity at all in which boys and girls, under the guise of horseplay or hostility, could lay eager hands upon each other's person. I know that when I first stumbled upon the back rub stratagem, during the heated summer of my sixteenth year, I thought I'd hit upon the most novel and ingenious ploy ever devised; my discovery, I felt, had instantly catapulted me into the ranks of Copernicus, Galileo, Newton. I tried, unsuccessfully, to take out a patent on it.

Before very long, however, everyone seemed to be in on my prized little secret. Back rubs, and massage in general, were a standard, even transparent, overture. If a guy wasn't bold enough to come right out and suggest making love, he crinkled up his shoulders, winced, and complained about his backache, hoping his date would volunteer to give him a rub-down. Or else he'd say to her, with great concern, something like, "Gee, you seem so tense tonight," laying one hand on the nape of her neck. "I can feel it, there's a knot right here in your neck and your shoulders. Can you feel it? Here," turning her away slightly, "you want me to work it out for you?"

The funny thing is, now that we're grown-ups, and can approach sex directly and with some candor, the back rub seems to have come back into style. It's being appreciated all over again, not so much as a cunning ruse—"Who doesn't know what it means by now?" asks Larry—but for its own inherent virtues. Now it's being incorporated into a lot of lovemaking bouts because, among other things, it happens to feel terrific.

"Jan used to be great at it," says my friend Mike, a wistful note in his voice. "She used to do it the same way she kissed, letting her hands roam all over me, from one spot to another, always sort of surprising me and always going exactly where I wanted her to, without my ever having to say a word." As with kisses, a gentle touch is hard to misplace.

But "gentle" is the all-important word there. A massage given for purposes of seduction is not the same as a massage given by a trained professional for therapeutic reasons. That distinction, I think, sometimes gets lost. Once, when I was briefly going out with a modern dancer, she persuaded me— not that it was very hard—to lie down and let her give me a massage. Eager to demonstrate all that she had learned about anatomy over eight years of dance classes, she proceeded to twist, pummel, pound, rend, and dislocate every bone, mus-cle, and fiber in my body. Not wanting to appear a wimp, I bit my lip and suffered in silence until, opening one eye and seeing my left leg now resting in the next room, I decided that I'd had enough relaxation for one session, rolled over and said, "Thanks so much, I could have you go on all night, but I feel too guilty about making you do all the work."

"Oh, that's okay," she assured me. "I *like* to do it. How do you feel now?"

"Words can't describe," I replied.

"Just let me do this one little pectoral exercise I know on you," she said, inching forward and extending her lethal hands toward my chest.

"*No*," I nearly shouted, bolting upright from my bed of pain. "That's really alright—*really*. I simply couldn't *stand* to have you exert yourself further. You've already done more than enough. Really." I clasped her hands safely between mine. "Let me do you now."

Then, as sensation gradually crept back into my damaged limbs, I gave her the kind of massage that I'd expected, and wanted, myself. Long, tender strokes up and down her body, soft pressure here and there, feather-light touches, occasionally punctuated by a quick smooch. I may not know any more about human anatomy than I've managed to pick up in the shower every morning, but I do know what feels good, and what doesn't.

Surprisingly enough, most other men do, too. Our problem is that we don't always know how to ask for what we want— particularly if what we want is simply to be babied, to be affectionately embraced, caressed, fondled. We don't know how to say, "Stroke me softly," "Touch me there," or, Heaven forbid, "Just hold me." Sex we know how to ask for; tender, loving care we're embarrassed to request.

That's where that massage can come in awfully handy. A man can get what he wants without expressly asking for it. And you, by carefully monitoring his sighs, smiles, and twitches, can figure out what he finds physically pleasurable. Though each man is going to have his own particularly sensitive spots, in other ways we're all alike—and to tell the truth, not all that different from you.

In both sexes, there are certain spots on the body where nerve endings tend to congregate, and where just a little bit of rubbing can go a long way toward arousal. The neck, for instance, or the ears, under the arms, or on the inside of the thighs. The buttocks are a good bet not because they're such a keen neurological focus (some buttocks can't tell polyester underwear from 100 percent cotton) but because they carry an erotic charge. A man's nipples, according to many books I've read, are another erogenous hot spot, though after asking around among all my friends, I have yet to find one who thinks his own are. "I have about as much feeling in my nipples," says Larry, "as I do in my gym shoes." That was the general consensus.

A couple of other pointers on massage: Use some baby oil, or some other kind of lotion, and warm it up in your hands before applying it to his body. Once you've begun, never take both your hands off his skin at the same time (it has an odd way of breaking the connection between you), and don't concentrate too much of your attention on just one or two areas—particularly if they're the erogenous zones. Instead, run your hands evenly all over him, from the soles of his feet to the tip of his cowlick. Don't miss a thing.

The advantage to such thoroughness will show up shortly. By sensitizing his entire body, you've subtly diffused his sexual current; you've re-channeled some of his ardor away from the genitals and into other forms of foreplay. And if there's any one problem that crops up time and again in the bedrooms of America, it's the way men have of vaulting over all the little niceties of sex, the kissing and nibbling and fondling, and into the actual act itself. A slow and sensual massage will give him time to relax and slow down, give you time to catch up and get cooking yourself, and prolong the lovemaking for both of you. And all for only $1.39, the price of a bottle of baby oil. Can you resist such a bargain?

Serious Business

If kissing and rubbing and other sorts of foreplay are considered the sexual hors d'oeuvres, then the problem that confronts you as a woman is this: Just how many of them can you serve a man without running the risk of his suddenly losing his "appetite," so to speak, prematurely, thereby abruptly bringing things to a halt?

There are certain telltale signs to be on the lookout for: Has he begun breathing at the rate of a Siberian husky on an August afternoon? Has he turned the color of your crimson window seat? Has he lost command of the English language? Is his entire body twitching convulsively, as if his big toe had been inserted in the light socket? These are all reliable, and medically sound, indicators of male sexual arousal. Watch for them.

Of course, the single most easily read barometer lies below, and though thousands of pages have already been written on what to do and what not to do when a penis comes knocking at your door, nearly all of it, I think, can be reduced to a couple of fairly simple principles. First of all, it's almost impossible to do wrong here; the penis is such a wildly egomaniacal creature that it will accept just about any kind of attention or accolade it can get. It questions nothing, and never reads between the lines. The most sensitive areas are the underside of the shaft and the head, and feathery strokings directed there will elicit anything from a contented sigh to the promise of a two-week, all-expenses paid vacation to the Côte d'Azur. (If you can, get that in writing.) Do not, however, confuse the delightful pliancy of the penis with an infinite elasticity; under your loving ministrations, it will indeed grow, but it will not grow indefinitely. Nor is its increasing firmness any indication of durability or resilience. Do not, for instance, attempt to see if it will scratch a diamond, or bounce back in place after a resounding thwack from your forefinger. It may, once, but your chances of seeing its owner again are as slim as a blizzard in June.

As to its size, any comment you choose to make had better be very carefully edited. Most men are kind of antsy about this topic, unsure if they measure up to the competition, and an unwitting remark like "Well, how's our little friend down there?" can create deep, psychic reverberations—and possibly detumescence. By and large, the less said about the penis, the better. If you feel, however, that you must speak out, you might try complimenting it on its aesthetic refinement, noble purity of line, or general air of distinction. And if it just so happens that what you're dealing with is manifestly one of Nature's most colossal specimens, a rampant miracle of hydraulic design and grandeur, then do feel free to say so.

"Just about the sexiest thing I can think of," said a friend of mine who threatened my life if I revealed his true identity, "is when the woman I'm living with helps me to unroll and put on a condom, and wonders out loud how this itsy-bitsy little rubber is ever going to be able to get all the way around me. It's almost a game at this point, just kind of a silly routine we go through, but I'd really miss it if it stopped."

Though I haven't actually asked him, I'm sure my anonymous friend wouldn't mind if you, too, decided to try out his little game. It's not only a fairly sensual idea in its own right, but it also solves some of the problems that men often have when using a condom: They don't like the notion of having to stop, right in the middle of making love, to unroll and pull it on, and sometimes the interruption can even be enough to cause them to lose their erection. If instead of lying quietly alongside him while he tussles with it in the dark, you lean over and make it part of what you do together (and after all, it is being done for both of you), the "interruption" may soon get to be one of the nicest parts of the whole shebang.

Some couples, I gather, even do the same thing when using a diaphragm. I say "I gather" because even though I've seen the notion of putting it in together recommended in various books and magazine articles, I have yet to turn up a single man among my own numerous acquaintances who wants to help out in this way. I know it ain't fair—I mean, why should he expect you to pitch in if he won't do the same?—but that's what I've discovered. I make no judgments; I only report the news. There is, however, one signal difference with the diaphragm, and that is, it *can* be put in some time beforehand, and privately. Which, until you've actually had a chance to discuss it with the man in your life to see how he feels about it, I suppose I'd recommend. But do try to schedule that discussion for some time *before* getting into bed.

In bed, there are plenty of other things to talk about. And no, I don't mean the weather (unless, of course, it happens to be unusually interesting that day). I mean tender things, sexy things, even, let us say, obscene things. Bandying about a bit of graphic chat is more than a good way of increasing your mutual arousal—it can actually help to iron out some persistent little difficulties you may be having.

This may not come as much of a surprise to you, but there are a pretty fair number of guys out there—decent, civilized, well-educated sorts—who still know next to nothing about the female body and what it enjoys. They operate on a kind of hit-or-miss system—if you don't actively object to whatever it is they're doing, they assume you've been transported on waves of bliss (when, in fact, you may simply have fallen asleep). If, on the other hand, you let out an ear-piercing shriek, then they know to cease and desist from whatever they've been up to. Anywhere in between, they don't entirely know how well they're doing.

Even I, yes, I myself, even me, have found myself baffled from time to time, particularly at the start of a new relationship, with a woman reluctant to express her proclivities and desires. I think by now I have a passable sense of where things are and how they work, but as every woman is different (dare I say, unique as every snowflake?) it's a great help to me if she'll drop at least a clue now and then to let me know, for instance, that she *doesn't* like to be coated with apricot jam, *does* like to be kissed on her collarbone, or *hates* having her hair chewed. Otherwise, how's a guy to know?

"I'd say I must have gone out with Kim for at least six months," says Gerald, "before I really knew what she liked in bed. It's not that I was doing anything all that wrong, you understand. It's just that I hadn't figured out the particular little things that she wanted me to do more of."

"Such as?" I inquired.

"You think I'm crazy enough to tell you?"

"No, I guess not," I replied, with a downcast look.

"The specifics aren't all that important anyway," he said, regretting already his brutal assault on me. "It's just that it took months and months before one night we got very stoned, went to bed, and started to tell each other all about the stuff we really liked, and what got us excited, and all of that."

"You mean you'd never really discussed it at all?"

"No, not with words. It was more a matter of nudging each other this way or that in the dark, or breathing heavily when something was being done right, or changing positions if something wasn't on target. Anything rather than having to say right out, 'I wish you'd move three inches to the left, darling,' or 'Do that one more time and I'll love you forever.'"

"Why do you think that was?" I said, pressing my luck still further.

"Embarrassment mostly. It's hard to know how and when to bring these things up. When you first start going to bed with someone, you don't want to be issuing all these instructions, or running through a catalogue of your sexual tastes. And then later, when you've been going out for awhile, you're afraid that you're going to hurt the other person's feelings by implying that maybe he or she hasn't been up to par so far. There's just no easy, or un-dangerous, way to discuss this stuff."

Agreed. But if *you*, in your role as an enlightened, independent, and self-confident twentieth-century woman, are able to take the lead and tactfully open up the subject, the man in your life will surely follow. And you'll be doing the both of you an enormous favor. No more missed signals in the dark, no more lingering frustration, no more silent, fervent wishing that he would only, just this once, be able to read your mind. Now you can simply speak it—while exercising, of course, a fair degree of diplomacy. Not, "You bumptious cretin, haven't you ever heard of removing your socks before getting in bed?"; but, "Honey cakes, sweetie pie, wouldn't you feel more comfortable if you took off those handsome argyle socks for just a little while? There now, we'll put them right here on the bedside table, so you can still see them. Isn't that better?" Once the socks are off, so to speak, you can talk about anything. And once you can do that, the sex, along with just about everything else in your life together, is bound to get even better.

Afterplay

The candles have burnt down to a bare nub, the bed is a holy mess, the two of you rest against the pillows, sated, your limbs loosely intertwined. Languidly, you extend one arm to the bedside table, push aside the argyles, retrieve your cigarettes and lighter. The flame glows for an instant, you draw on the cigarette, send a thin curl of smoke spiraling toward the ceiling. Your pulse is just beginning to slow down.

"Alex, that was wonderful."

He makes no reply.

"Really . . . just wonderful." You turn your head toward him. "Did you enjoy it?" Of course he enjoyed it, you say to yourself, he bellowed like a water buffalo. But still he doesn't say anything. "Alex, was it good for you?" You can't believe you've just said that, but there it is. "Alex?" you repeat, with some concern now. "Are you okay?"

From somewhere deep in the folds of the pillow, where his face is now largely buried, you think you hear . . . yes, you did hear . . . there's no mistaking it now . . . a snore! The callous boor has gone to sleep! He's just run through 36 chapters of the Kama Sutra with you, he's enjoyed the four-star soufflé you made for dinner, he's been rubbed and oiled and kissed and coddled, and this is the way he shows his gratitude! By expending himself, and nodding off. You have to fight an overpowering urge to stub out your cigarette on his slumbering rump.

But stop—let me, if I may, say a few words on behalf of the defenseless Alex, and all the other men who have slipped straight from sexual bliss into the beckoning arms of Morpheus. I've been known to do it myself, and that's why I can, and must, assure you that we do not mean to be unkind, or thoughtless, or rude. It's absolutely no reflection on the woman we're with, nor is it an oblique comment on her soufflés, sensuality, or skills as a masseuse. It's just that we've got this little trigger in our bodies, that right after orgasm releases a chemical, which in turn puts us to sleep. Much as we'd like to resist its pull, there are times when the temptation is too great, the sensation too delicious, our exhaustion too complete, and we succumb. Resist the urge to use us as an ashtray, give us a few minutes to indulge in our drugged sleep, and I promise, we'll revive ourselves very shortly.

When we do manage to swim back up into consciousness, we'll be grateful for the rest, suitably responsive and affectionate again, and in many instances, dying for a snack. I don't know what it is about sex that makes me desperate for something lethally sweet, but I know I'm not alone in this predilection. If you haven't already served dessert earlier in the evening, then this is the time to break out something really glutinous and delectable, a sacher torte or a baba au rhum. Sprinkle liberally with cinnamon and sugar, cover with chocolate chips, drench in honey, and you're talking business. Syrup is optional, according to taste.

Part V

Parting Shots

On Breaking Up

Relationships, viewed philosophically, are a lot like fruit—from a tiny seed, they grow, get sweeter, fuller, achieve, for a fleeting moment, their ultimate ripeness, and then, quite imperceptibly, begin their decay. Before you know it, you've got a sour mush on your hands, which all you can do is throw out.

Please don't misunderstand me—I don't believe _all_ relationships go bad. I'm not so cynical as that. I only wish to observe that before you hit on that perfect union, that bond so strong and true it can last a lifetime (and I _do_ believe they exist) you'll probably have to go through a whole binfull of relationships that don't work out. You'll wind up, unavoidably, investing a lot of time and effort in love affairs that, once they're behind you, you'll wryly refer to as "learning experiences." And you'll probably wish you could have skipped some of the lessons along the way.

What _makes_ a relationship go bad? What stealthy and sinister forces are at play, working to corrupt our hopes of perfect felicity? Who can say—whatever they are, they're as subtle as the Mona Lisa's smile, as varied as the shades of nail polish on the first floor of Bloomingdale's. No matter how many "learning experiences" you've already chalked up, each time a new relationship starts to crumble it's for different reasons, and under different circumstances. Sometimes the precipitating factor is fairly blatant and prosaic: "I got home to find him in bed with my best friend." Sometimes it's more esoteric: "She had to consult the _I Ching_ before doing anything, from choosing a blouse to brushing her teeth." Sometimes a mountain seems to have been made of a molehill: "She was always tying up the telephone line." Sometimes a mountain seems to have been made of a mountain: "He was running an international cocaine-smuggling ring out of _my_ apartment." The surface problems are never that hard to discover; what's much tougher is figuring out the real, underlying causes for the friction.

"For the last year or so that Kim and I were together," says my friend Gerald, "we were squabbling about one thing or another nearly all the time, from where to go to dinner, to what color wallpaper to put up in the bathroom. It was only after we'd broken up, and I had a lot of time to seriously think about it, that I realized what the biggest problem had been all along. Kim's background was . . . I don't know, what would you call one rung below blue collar? Whereas I came from your typical overprivileged suburban background. We were both just starting to get successful at our respective jobs, and while I had no conflicts about that whatsoever, Kim did—she was very reluctant to get ahead, very unsure of herself. In retrospect, I can see that she was fighting 'upward mobility' every step of the way, and though I couldn't have formulated it at the time, I think I *felt* that she was trying, without even knowing it herself, to hold me back, too. I just think we were starting to pull in opposite directions by the end there."

"My problem was really timing more than anything else," says Peter. "The woman I was seeing was seven years older than I am, and even though that isn't all that much of a difference, it got to the point where she was tired of the whole 'dating scene' and wanted to settle down, have a baby, all that, and I just wasn't ready yet. I needed a few more years of running around first."

And then there's my friend Linda, who still isn't entirely sure why she broke up with her boyfriend, Buddy. She's the first to concede he was kind, sensitive, thoughtful, generous, honest, trusting, gentle. . . . "That's what drives me crazy. I have almost nothing to complain about in Buddy—he's a wonderful, wonderful person. But after two years of going out with him, I still simply wasn't in love, and I knew that I never would be. That elusive chemistry," she concludes, regretfully, "simply was not there."

Sometimes, that's all you *can* say. The reasons people drift apart are generally as mysterious as the reasons they come together. Sometimes, the break-up is abruptly declared, with a shout and a slammed door, by only one party; more often, it's a resolution reluctantly reached, and agreed upon, by both parties. In either case, it's been cooking for awhile, and the signs, whether you happened to notice them or not, were there all along.

Trouble Brewing

"Dumb as this is probably going to sound," said my friend Larry, "what really made me sit up and notice something was wrong between Meg and me was when she took a shower one night and came into the bedroom, just wrapped in a towel, to get ready for bed. What I realized, after we'd turned out the light, was that I'd been flipping through the cartoons in *The New Yorker* the whole time, and for the first time I could recall, I hadn't looked up to watch her take her towel off, or pull on her nightie. I'm *not* 85 years old—I didn't think that should have been happening yet. It really made me wonder, as I lay there in the dark, if something hadn't gone out of the relationship."

It's almost always something as trivial as that—a towel not snatched away, a kiss goodbye forgotten at the door—that suddenly gives you pause, that makes you stop and wonder if everything is exactly as it should be. It's finding yourself in the midst of the third heated argument in one week, this time over which party to attend that coming Saturday; it's getting good news and not rushing to the phone to inform your lover of it before everyone else; it's shopping for a birthday gift and settling for the first thing you see, instead of running all over town to find something really special. It's waking up in the morning on opposite sides of the bed, your backs turned to each other. It's any such minor detail as these that can bring you up short, that can point out to you, in an unwelcome flash, the writing on the wall.

Sometimes, with some immediate work, some serious soul-searching and painfully honest conversation, the writing can be expunged, the relationship set back on the proper course again. But much of the time, the writing reappears, the same old problems crop up over and over, until you finally have to concede that the differences between you are irreconcilable, that the glue now holding you both together is made up less of devotion than sorrow, and the fears that any separation entails.

"I broke up with Buddy so many times that I got embarrassed to tell my friends about it anymore," says Linda. "I was the girl who'd cried wolf too many times. It's just that every time we had one of our break-ups, I'd feel so heart-broken and depressed and weepy that I'd call him back a few days later, and we'd decide to try again, and the whole thing would start all over—until I reached that inevitable point where I realized once again that no, I still wasn't in love with him."

Perhaps the trickiest thing about breaking up is that it does feel so much like love—all the sadness and regret and, yes, affection that wells up at the very thought of parting with someone you've been close to, all the fears of loneliness and starting over, conspire together to create a very close facsimile of real honest-to-goodness love. Tears make it hard enough to see the feeling for what it really is—our desires make it even harder. We want so much to believe in it, we're so eager to find a way out of our grief, that we clutch at this sudden heart-surge like a last-minute reprieve . . . when all we've really done is postpone the day of reckoning.

Which isn't to say that the "serial separation" is necessarily a bad bit of strategy. Breaking up is hard to do (to coin a phrase), and going through a few "rehearsals," painful as they are, can sometimes make it easier in the end. Each time, we're a little more resolved, a little more aware, a lot wearier. And since we're never entirely sure if this particular break-up is going to be the one to take or not, some of the sting is gone. Knowing that we might very well wind up back together again can be a fortifying thought—so fortifying, in fact, that it can help us to avoid doing just that. And eventually, one of the separations has got to stick.

Can't We Still Be Friends?

Even after the break-up, however, there's likely to be a strong temptation to act in what is commonly thought an adult and sophisticated fashion, to show yourselves and the world that no rancor exists, by managing that magical feat of "staying friends." It's a nice idea, an enlightened idea, but not, to my way of thinking, a very *good* idea.

As a tragic case in point, let me cite my own relationship with Alice, which ended in a reasonably amicable fashion. We'd been together for a couple of years, but for some time had been flying in that proverbial holding pattern, both of us aware that we weren't actually going anywhere, and that if we tried to we'd only discover we were headed in altogether different directions. We knew it in our hearts long, long before we were willing to admit it openly, to each other or to ourselves.

Once we *did* acknowledge the awful truth, we decided, in all our profound naïveté, that there was no purpose in rashly junking the whole relationship—we'd simply open it up, you see, spend less time with each other, start dating other people when we felt like it. This first stage (in what would ultimately prove a three-stage process) lasted until the day I called her to say I'd accepted a dinner party invitation for us and she said she'd already accepted a date for that same night. Quite apart from all logistical questions, I abruptly discovered that I wasn't yet ready for the sophisticated, mature, "open relationship"—and the poor woman I did take to that party will probably never know why I looked like a condemned man all evening.

As our next step, Alice and I agreed that "opening" the relationship, while continuing to sleep together every so often, had clearly been attempting the impossible—at least for us. If we were going to be friends, then we had better be just that, friends. With no fooling around.

Well, in *theory*, that was all well and good. We just naturally assumed that our abiding affection for each other, our mutual concern, our common interests, our friends, would all provide a sustaining bond between us. And after all, we thought, wasn't it the other *person*, and not his or her corporeal being, that we'd loved all along anyway?

Guess what—it *was* the corporeal being, at least to the extent that it couldn't be separated out from the more "spiritual" component of our relationship. I mean, let's face it—if there *weren't* some mystically, chemically, *physical* element at work in these affairs of the heart, we'd all be just as content to smooch with our friends. And we're not.

At this point, reluctantly, Alice and I had to concede that just laying eyes on each other—even over drinks in a crowded restaurant—was too hard to handle. It only stirred up those carefully banked fires, and made us wonder anew whether it wasn't possible, somehow, to return to the comfort, the security, even the passion, of our best days together. It's amazing, how easily a couple of warming cocktails can obliterate the recollection of the anger, frustration, ennui, that you once felt. Especially on those days when the world has been unkind and the urge to curl up in the cosmic lap is virtually irresistible.

So now we were left with only one recourse—the telephone—if we wished to maintain our drowning "friendship," clearly about to go down for the third and last time. And for many months, we did stay on the phone, struggling to make small talk while scrupulously avoiding large talk, until, slowly and very unsurely, week by week, we eventually managed to wean ourselves away from that tempting receiver, and each other.

And it was only *then* that I truly began to feel open again to the possibility of a new romance, receptive to the idea of a new woman in my life. That may not sound like much, I suppose—but I think where there's still a kind of psychic attachment to a previous love, there's also an unconscious impulse to sabotage a new one. Without meaning to, you make constant comparisons between your past lover and your present date, an unfair contest if ever there was one. How on earth could someone who's known you for two hours be expected to read your mood, appreciate your sense of humor, understand your sensitivities, as well as someone who spent two years at it? And frankly, why should he or she care to yet?

It's only when you can give that new person a fair chance that you give yourself a fair one, too—it's only when you've really committed yourself to finding a "next" relationship that you'll be able to pull it off. Breaking up is comparatively a cinch—it's staying that way, especially over those first few cold and lonely months, that calls on every ounce of your moral fiber; it's forcing yourself to remember the pain and the reasons for breaking up in the first place; it's realizing, and finally *accepting*, that you won't ever find that new true love—and there *will* be one, you have to believe that—until you've made the heart-rending decision, finally and irrevocably, to be done with the old.

Unfortunately, trying to "stay friends" will almost undoubtedly make starting over just that much harder (unless, of course, you parted on the most awful terms, in which case you won't want to anyway). There *is* a pretty fair chance that, if time and circumstance throw you together at some further remove, at a time when both of you have gone on to new, satisfying relationships, you will be able to become friends, of sorts. I keep up with a couple of my old flames from college days, and even one from high school, but all those fires are safely out now. We have settled into other lives, with other companions, and there's no longer any undeniable current between us.

I do wish I could say that "staying friends" is a great and workable idea, an idea whose time has at long last come, but I just don't think that's the case. Nor, to be perfectly honest, do I see much chance that it ever will be—at least not until somebody's come up with a much more sensible model for the always eccentric, and thoroughly unpredictable, human heart.

Full Speed Ahead!

While we're waiting for that miracle of invention to come along, there do happen to be an interesting assortment of smaller, more easily accomplished, things we can do to help us get over those lovesick blues. Do you sit home nights with the television, two radios, the vacuum cleaner, and your Water-Pik on, just to escape the silence of your own four walls? Do you sleep until noon, get up to feed the cat, and then crawl back under the covers? Do you call your friends to give them hourly bulletins, in 25,000 words or less, on how you're feeling about the break-up now? Do you concoct for yourself breathtaking ice cream sundaes, which you consume, wearing a faded bathrobe (the one you'd never let him see you in), while listening to plaintive James Taylor songs and idly looking back over all the good times you'd had together. Do you start to think, maybe the bad times weren't so bad after all, maybe he could be *cured* of his shoe fetish, maybe six years hadn't really been giving it a fair shot, maybe you'd been unwittingly cruel that night, showing no interest in his Japanese dung-beetle collection. . . . Do you, half-consciously, watch the telephone, waiting for it to ring, and wondering what you'd say to a suggested rapprochement?

If you didn't do at least *some* of these things, you'd be a subject for case-book study; if you didn't wallow for at least a few days, you'd be worthy of a place in the Guinness Book of World Records. I for one believe strongly in the value of a good wallow; I hate all that stiff-upper-lip stuff. If you're feeling a little blue—say, robin's egg blue—and you feel like giving into it, go ahead. Go all the way to navy if you like. Mope around the house for a weekend, thumb through the photos of a happier time, listen to "Sweet Baby James" if you think you can stand it. Have a sundae.

But once you've spent a few days in the slough of despond, once you've effectively put your heart and soul through the wringer, there does come a time to toss off the bathrobe, make the bed, and rinse out the ice cream bowl. Even if you have no particular place to go that day, even if it's just another gray and lazy Sunday, don't get into your most "comfy" outfit—put on something a little more special, something you think looks positively attractive on you. (An evening gown, with pearls, and matching pumps, is perhaps a bit much.)

Spruce yourself up, so that catching a glimpse of yourself in the bedroom mirror will be a beautiful and rewarding experience.

Then tackle your apartment. And I don't mean just dusting off the bookshelves and washing the windows (though once when I did mine, I was astonished to discover I live facing the front); what I'm suggesting is that you make a scrupulous and methodical search of your premises, and to the best of your abilities, ferret out each and every reminder of your ex-sweetie. The stuff that isn't so valuable as to warrant keeping—an old sock, a dog-eared copy of *You and Your Power Saw,* a frazzled toothbrush—consign to the garbage; the rest of the stuff, things you might want to keep, like letters, photos, the hand-tooled bookmark he brought you from Portugal, deposit in a cardboard box. Stash the box on the uppermost shelf of your least-used closet. Try to forget that it's there.

Depending on the state of your finances, and your heart, you may even decide to pull out all the stops and redecorate the old place. Not only will it give you something to occupy your mind, but the change in decor may signal to you, in a pleasant and reassuring way, the change in your life, too. (If, however, you find yourself leaning toward black walls, smoked-glass mirrors, and framed photographs by Diane Arbus, hold off; you may not be sufficiently recovered yet.) I know that after I broke up with Alice it took me three months before I even realized that one of the things keeping me depressed was a painting she'd done, that had been hanging over my bed for so long I hardly noticed it was there anymore. Replacing it with a nice, noncommittal lithograph helped a lot.

But my friends, more than anything else, really did the trick. They helped take me out of myself, not to mention out of my apartment, and they gave me, in a perfectly effortless, uncomplicated fashion, a healthy measure of the warmth and affection that anyone just getting over an affair so desperately needs. Kicking a love habit is a lot like kicking any other addiction—sometimes the temporary "fix" is absolutely essential.

That, and the gumption to go out there and try again! One good thing about breaking up is that once it's over, you know that you can live through it; the worst that can happen is still survivable. With that in mind, there should be nothing to stop you from throwing on your finery and taking off for the first party you hear of. Just do be sure, before leaving the house, that you haven't foolishly put on new underwear, or too conspicuously tidied up the place. Because, in case you've forgotten, the gods who appear to preside over these romantic matters like nothing better than to foil an optimist. Don't let 'em know that you're back on the prowl, until it's too late and you've already found your next great passion.

About the Author

Robert Masello is a bachelor, a native of Chicago, and a graduate of Princeton. In addition to two published books, he writes frequently for such magazines as *New York, Travel & Leisure* and *Town and Country.* For the past three years, he's been featured monthly in *Mademoiselle,* where "*His,*" a column dispensing friendly advice on matters of romantic interest, inspires a steady stream of fan mail. Mr. Masello is a frequent speaker on the college circuit and currently resides on Manhattan's fashionable East Side.